Your Legacy: Meaningful Estate Planning

Second Edition

Steven R. Owens, J.D.

Your Legacy: Meaningful Estate Planning

Manufactured in the United States of America

Library of Congress Cataloging-in-Publication data is on file with
the publisher

ISBN13 (paperback, 2nd edition) 978-0-9816583-9-1

Book design by Louise Gaillard, One Stop Books

Dedication

My dedication to creating true legacies is shaped in large part by my parents, both because they set a great example by creating their own wonderful legacies, and also because they insisted on seeing only the best work from their children. With sincere thanks to my mother, Patricia M. Owens, I am dedicating this book to the memory of my father, John R. Owens, whose admonition, "If it is worth doing, it is worth doing right!" still rings in my ears as an important part of his own unique and meaningful legacy.

Acknowledgments

Every reference book is actually a collaboration—we authors draw upon what we have learned from others—and I want to acknowledge and thank all of my professors, instructors, mentors and colleagues who, over the years, have helped me understand how to create a true legacy for my clients.

This book is even more of a collaboration, because portions of the First Edition were contributed or reviewed by my good friends and colleagues at the Education Forum: Karen Brady, Justin Dituri, Steve Gammill, Joel Keith and Peter Scott. I especially benefitted from Karen Brady's contributions and comments for this Second Edition. Of course, the responsibility for the content of this book is mine alone.

Over the years I have had the privilege of working with talented staff, and I want to thank my current team, Carey Norrish and Teresa Mitchell, for their devotion to our clients and their assistance in the creation of this book.

I also want to thank my children, John, Thomas and Phillip, for creating in me a personal awareness of the importance of creating a meaningful legacy. Most importantly of all, I want to thank my wonderful wife Rachelle, who not only helped me through law school, but has assisted me ever since then in more ways that I ever could count as we created our family law practice, and who has been my best friend, my true love and my rock of support for all these years.

Foreword

When I began helping my clients with their estate planning, more than 20 years ago, I turned to the typical reference resources that attorneys consult. Those books were almost exclusively driven by tax and legal concerns, and gave very short shrift to the family and human concerns. These books are the reason that most estate plans look alike, and that most estate plans have one formula for distribution of your hard-earned wealth to children (… 1/3 at age 25, 1/3 at age 30, and 1/3 at age 35…).

This just didn't seem right! My clients were all different, their children and other loved ones were all different (most of them were already over 35), and I just could not understand how the one-size-fits-all plans that most estate planners were using could be appropriate for all of these very different families.

So I went on a quest: I went to all of the estate planning workshops, symposiums, and seminars that I could find, so that I could learn how create unique plans for my clients, and how I could make their plans work more efficiently than "standard" estate plans, which usually required a probate proceeding and often required the payment of taxes.

Then the real journey began: I had to learn how to listen carefully to my clients, since their deepest wishes are often the ones that they are reluctant to share. I had to learn to listen for that hesitation that indicated that perhaps, just perhaps, their daughter had some unmentioned marital problems and that deep in their hearts they wanted to protect her legacy: "lets talk about that." Or perhaps their son had a mild disability that caused my clients to worry about whether they should put some stronger protections on his legacy: "lets talk about that." Or perhaps they wanted to create a legacy for their grandchildren, but didn't really know exactly what they wanted that legacy to be: "lets talk about your grandchildren—what would you really like to ensure for them?"

I let my clients teach me about all of the wonderful, unique, and meaningful legacies they wanted to put in place, but never dreamed were possible. I can assure you, that they are all possible, those plans, more than a thousand, are now in place, and this book is about how you can begin your own journey of determining how your wealth will affect the lives of your loved ones, how you will be remembered, how you will create a meaningful legacy.

Obviously, laws, regulations, techniques and challenges will change over time. I have incorporated all of the changes in the law into this Second Edition, so it is fully up to date today. However, I am sure that the laws will continue to change over time, so to see if anything set forth in this book needs to be updated, please visit my website *www.mydenverlawyer.com* and select the "Book Updates" icon where you will find the most recent updates, revisions and additions to this book.

With that in mind, let your journey begin…

TABLE OF CONTENTS

INTRODUCTION

This book is intended to educate, but it is also intended to provoke thought and action. You can find many books on estate planning. Yet there are no other books with the same approach to planning as this one. The approach presented here emphasizes your individual personal goals over the technicalities. The approach set forth in this book recognizes that your legacy consists of much more than your money. It also assumes that estate planning is essentially about care and concern for others. It is this concern about family, friends, and communities that motivates people to plan for a future that extends beyond a single lifetime.

Just as your legacy is about more than just your property, the art and science of estate planning is about much more than just the tools of wills, taxes, probate, or trusts. Of course, this book covers those topics. Knowledge of how these tools work allows you to be an effective participant in your estate planning. However, that knowledge is only the means to an end, or steps towards your ultimate goal. That goal will be different for each and every person. In addition to showing you how to put your legacy into place, this book will help you begin to identify your own goals.

Your estate planning team will also be an important resource in identifying and reaching your goals. Choosing the right attorney, financial advisor, and tax professional will make the estate planning process more effective and much less stressful for you. In addition to the necessary technical knowledge, these professionals should be able and willing to counsel you in clarifying your goals and choosing the approach to meet those goals in a way that fits you and the people and things that matter to you. While many attorneys and other advisors will profess to have perfected an estate plan, beware of any one-size-fits-all approach. As opposed to that one-size-fits-all approach, the advisors that I work with and my team believe that the true value of your estate planning team lies in the counseling they provide to you, and the opportunities that they explain to you, and the value does not lie simply in the resulting estate planning documents.

Therefore, estate planning should be understood to be a process. An effective estate plan is not a static item that you complete once in your lifetime and then consider to be finished. Like a financial plan, business plan, or household budget, it is something that must be implemented and re-evaluated. The right estate planning team will help you implement your plan. At a minimum, that will mean understanding the legacy plan that you have created, and then titling your assets and naming your beneficiaries in accordance with that plan. However, it usually means much more than that. It also means making sure that your assets are invested appropriately to meet the goals of your plan. It means ensuring that complete and accurate records are kept and tax returns are filed. It may also involve purchasing insurance. These are all areas in which your team of advisors must be well-versed.

The estate planning process often involves more than what appears on your balance sheet. It can involve documenting your personal values and philosophy. It may include finding ways to pass on the stories that communicate the value of things, people, places, and communities that are important to you. I have found that these will have great meaning to those who will follow you.

The process is ongoing. The factors you considered most important in the initial phase of your estate planning will change over time. There may be external changes, such as changes in the law or available financial products. There will also be internal changes that affect your family, your assets, and your own life. All of these changes require re-evaluation, and often an amendment to your plan. Your estate planning team can help you determine the best way to approach this process to keep your plan current.

In the end, it is your life, your concerns and your desire to control the shape of your legacy that motivates you to create a legacy plan. This book is intended to help you understand what affects those concerns, so that the final result of the estate planning process can truly be called *your* legacy plan.

PART I: DISCERNING AND DEFINING YOUR GOALS

Chapter 1

- Your Goals Define Your Plan -

Why is goal setting important in estate planning?

If you think about planning a vacation, you probably think about several steps. You may start with choosing your destination. You'll think about when you want to travel. There will be other choices, such as where you'll stay or what activities you'll do. But underlying all of these choices are your goals for the vacation. Do you want to experience something new or focus on relaxation? Will it be a time for family bonding or individual pursuits? Your goals for your vacation determine whether you will travel by plane or by car or take a bicycle tour, but you won't consider the plan done just because you've packed the car or bought the plane tickets.

Planning your estate is like planning your vacation. Your goals for the plan dictate all of your other decisions. Just as your vacation is more than the car or plane you use to get there, your estate plan is more than the will or trust or the documents you use. You have to establish your goals for your plan so you know what you want it to accomplish. These goals dictate the documents and particulars of your plan.

It follows then that defining your goals and objectives and learning what each really means to you is important. Discover where your heart is as well as where your pocketbook is. It also can be a lot of fun. Often, people with very little money or tangible assets become every bit as enchanted with this process as people with significant financial resources.

Discover what is truly important to you and what you'd like to see happen. Most of us would be hard pressed to sit down and define our goals and objectives beyond a short version of an obvious: "I don't want my property to pass to the state and I don't want my three children fighting over it."

A really good travel agent will help you hone your vacation goals to have a trip of a lifetime. A really good lawyer will help you discern your estate planning goals to reflect what defines your life, to perpetuate your legacy. Just as your life is about more than your money, your estate plan is about more than distributing your assets at death.

Throughout this book you will learn the value of selecting the right lawyer, and you'll be introduced to how you might go about it. If you recognize the importance of goal setting and realize that,

- your true goals may be buried beneath the surface,
- you are going to need skilled help in pulling them up, and
- the importance of being able to articulate them, especially when some of them appear to conflict with others.

What does this have to do with creating a legacy?

Understanding and determining your goals is part and parcel of legacy planning and the extent to which one is included in the other depends greatly on your interest in leaving a legacy.

According to the Oxford dictionary, the word "legacy" is simply defined as: "a thing left to someone in a will, or handed down by a predecessor." Synonyms in that dictionary include: "a bequest, heritage, inheritance, patrimony."

This definition probably does not surprise you. Nor will it surprise you that most of us think of that definition in terms of money or property. The money you leave to your grandchildren is part of your legacy.

Sometimes a legacy is thought of as your reputation. *"He was always helping someone out. That was his legacy."*

Your legacy will consist of more than just what you plan to do with your property. It definitely includes all of "who you are" and how you choose to disclose that to those who come after you.

No two people will have the same goals and objectives once they have spent a little time thinking on the subject. That is why your legacy will be your own *unique* legacy.

How do I go about discovering and articulating my goals?

It isn't hard, but it takes some time. Unfortunately, some estate planning attorneys are not willing to devote that time. If the lawyer doesn't initiate the process, it will not happen. That is why your selection of the right attorney is important.

Once understood, the process is really straightforward and simple. It involves asking questions that are designed to encourage and entice you into telling stories about who you are, where you have been and what is important to you.

People who truly want an estate plan that reflects who they are, and how they want their children or heirs to receive their legacies, should seek estate planning professionals who share this philosophy. The result can be a glorious experience and a top-notch estate plan. Some say anything less than this is a plan that won't work or, at best, won't satisfy. Some disagree. The important point is for each person to explore and investigate.

How can I use this book to help create my legacy?

This book isn't a how-to book on creating a legacy. Before you build a house, you need to understand the site where it is to be built and the tools you can use. This book is about the lay of the land and the tools available for you to use in creating an estate plan that meets your goals. It's about common legacy concerns and how estate planning can solve them. When you learn about these things, you can then work with your lawyer to craft an estate plan that meets your unique legacy goals.

Chapter 2

- Loved Ones with Poor Judgment or Poor Financial Skills -

Can't I just leave everything equally to my six children?

The answer to that is "Yes!" Perhaps the better question is, "Do you want to?" Are all of your children equal? Are their needs the same? Are their expectations the same? Are their individual gifts, skills and talents equal or close to the same? The answer to all of those questions is typically a very loud "No!"

Remember, we are still talking about goals and legacies. You are learning what your goals are, how to articulate them, and how to create your own legacy. Most people, when first walking into the lawyer's office, simply assume they are going to leave their assets equally to their "six" children. If there is a "special needs child," one who has mental or physical disabilities that require special care, that one issue may be foremost in the mind of a parent. A few people are even aware that if they have a loved one on Medicaid or other governmental assistance programs, they will need to be careful not to leave money to those loved ones in a way that might disqualify that loved one from eligibility for the programs.

Many people are aware that their unique goals and objectives might call for something other than a direct and equal distribution to each of their children. More often than not, though, this is not the case and most people just haven't thought about some of the things to be discussed in this Section.

Most people have not spent any time thinking, *"My children are not equal kids."* As an example, consider a hypothetical family:

Son One: Dandy Don likes to live high on the hog. He is unmarried and his lifestyle is, to say the least, expensive. It just seems that whenever he gets a little money, whether from Dad or from his paycheck, it is immediately gone. Dandy Don is always driving a new car or on his way to somewhere like Hawaii.

Daughter One: Subservient Sue is married to a really wonderful man, but he is a little controlling. He has been married before and he has a couple of children from that marriage. He makes all the money decisions in the family — not only the spending decisions, but also what savings and investment programs will be undertaken. Subservient Sue always agrees with whatever her husband wants to do.

Son Two: Blessed Bobby and his wife Snow Queen are really what you would call free spirits. They are comfortably employed and they make a pretty good living. But there doesn't seem to be much to show for it. It is not because they don't know any better. It is really because they do not care. They contribute to good charitable causes (and some that might not be so worthwhile). They just want to make the world a better place. It is a good thing they have their health and, one might say, it's a good thing the world has them.

Son Three: Lucky Larry just won the lotto! He and his wife have four children and one on the way. Mom has watched him with money all his life and, while generally she approves of his spending habits and his lifestyle, he has never had this much before. She thinks there is a chance there won't be much left for his kids when he and his wife are through with it.

These are four very different and very unequal children. Mom and Dad really don't know what is going to happen in the future with these children and grandchildren. It is probably impossible to be definitive about how they want to distribute their estate among these young people. And, of course, Mom and Dad hope that their children won't still be young people when the time comes for them to receive Mom and Dad's legacy. Who will they be in five years, in twenty-five years? Will everyone still be healthy or will some be dealing with lifetime disabilities?

Speaking of disability, should I be concerned about my own?

Absolutely you should. When you become mentally or physically disabled to the point that you can no longer make your own decisions, your world changes for everybody involved, not just for you. There are two important areas to consider in this regard. The first has to do with your own personal situation. Questions like,

- "Who will determine if I'm disabled?"
- "When I am disabled how is my money to be spent?"
- "How do I want to be cared for at that time, and afterwards?"
- "Who's going to be taking care of me?"

A common response to the question about who will be making your decisions is, "My spouse, of course, will be taking care of me and he/she knows all the answers." What if your spouse cannot do it? What if he or she has been in a nursing home for the past five years, or if he or she was disabled or killed in the same automobile accident that disabled you?

In discussing this point, our hypothetical Mom and Dad quickly recognize that of these four children:

- None of them know Dad's wishes at this time,
- Dad will only be comfortable if he knows that a particular one of them will be taking care of him, and
- Dad absolutely does not want one of them to be in charge.

Mom discovers she has similar concerns.

The second area of concern is the changing needs of the four loved ones if Mom and Dad are no longer able to recognize those changes and to deal with them in the estate plan.

For example, assume that after Dad and Mom have become disabled, Son Two, Blessed Bobby, becomes ill and his illness is progressive. He genuinely needs some financial help but the estate plan did not take this possibility into account so there is no way to accommodate his needs. Because the decision makers, Mom and Dad, are disabled, the estate plan can't be changed at that time—if Mom and Dad want someone to be able to adjust their planning, then that flexibility must be built in from the beginning.

Can we make estate plans more flexible in anticipation of the unexpected?

Fortunately, estate planning professionals are spending more time talking with people about these issues than was typical in the past. More and more people are designing high levels of flexibility into their estate plans. Some are creating what are called "dynasty trusts." That is a trust designed to last more than one or two generations. Trustees (trusted people who manage the property and assets in the trust) are given greater latitude in deciding whether or not to make a distribution to a beneficiary. This kind of flexibility allows for greater asset protection and for distributions to beneficiaries that meet the beneficiary's needs and the times as they change (see Chapter 16, Protecting Future Generations ~ Dynasty Trusts).

Once you recognize that your children are not equal, you will appreciate the importance of thinking carefully how you want each to receive his or her inheritance. Some attorneys call that "Wealth Reception Planning."

What is Wealth Reception Planning?

It is nothing more than a new way to visualize your children and the legacies you will leave to them. It is an important component in the goals and legacy discussion.

Picture yourself at the time each child receives an inheritance from you and decide if you are comfortable with the way you have provided for that inheritance to pass to the child.

If, for example, Dandy Don is likely going to go through his money the way he presently does, then it is certainly possible he could have one or more very serious creditors hanging around just waiting for him to inherit. That possibility makes a difference when a parent thinks about how Dandy is going to receive his inheritance. Maybe Mom and Dad will decide to leave all or part of his inheritance in a trust that he cannot access except to the extent necessary to meet his needs. The creditors can not reach the inheritance. Mom and Dad may even decide to define for him what they believe those needs are or ought to be.

There is a principle of law here that needs to be understood. In layman's language, if Dandy has the legal ability to demand a distribution from a trust, then so does Dandy's creditor. If Mom and Dad want Dandy's creditor to be unable to reach the assets, then they may want to consider placing the distribution decisions in the hands of someone other than Dandy, an independent trustee. If that is done, Dandy can't make a demand on that trustee that he can enforce, therefore, neither can his creditor.

Consider as another example that Dandy decides to get married and that he and his wife later realize the marriage was a mistake. One or both of them may decide to divorce. How do the parents feel about Dandy's share of *their* money being given to this ex-wife by the divorce court?

Estate planning in today's day and age either does or should start with a careful understanding of Mom and Dad's goals and objectives regarding these types of concerns.

As noted earlier and emphasized through this Chapter, the first step is to learn what your goals really are and to recognize that some of these goals will be contingent or will be "it depends."

Then you must be able to actually articulate those goals and objectives. Once you have completed that important first step, the designing and implementing of a quality estate plan should be fairly easy for a qualified attorney.

Remember the most basic and important principle of estate planning: your estate plan is your plan, not the lawyer's. While that sounds simplistic, some attorneys truly believe that they know better than you do what is best for you and your loved ones. It is seldom true. While a good attorney certainly does understand the legal-technical aspects of planning and what is necessary to comply with the tax laws, he or she rarely knows your heart, your children, your goals and your objectives better than you. The best estate planning lawyers are going to first form a thorough understanding of who you are and what is most important to you. Then that lawyer is going to give you some options, some choices, as to how to make your personal and unique goals and objectives a reality. After listening to and being taught by the good lawyer, *you* should make the decisions. It truly is *your* estate plan.

Given they are so different, how do I provide maximum protection to each of my loved ones?

As you will see in the following Chapters, it is very possible to protect your loved ones and your legacy from predators, creditors, lawsuits and divorce court judges, as well as from the sticky fingers of Uncle Sam's IRS. However, in order to achieve maximum protection, you will need to exercise a fair level of control over your legacy.

It might be useful to compare this to a teeter-totter. Imagine that on one end of the teeter-totter is the concept of protection of the beneficiary's legacy. On the other end of the teeter- totter is the concept of the beneficiary's access to the legacy. Just like on the playground, when one side of the teeter-totter goes up, the other must come down. If you increase the access to the wealth: for example, if you say something in the trust like: "and Freddy Beneficiary shall have unlimited access to the property in the trust at age 35," you will have raised the access side of the teeter-totter and thus the protection side of the teeter-totter must fall. In other words, the wealth in the trust will have essentially no asset protection after Freddy reaches the age of 35, and the legacy will be exposed to creditors, lawsuit judgments, divorce court judges, etc., on that day. In addition, the Legacy will, on Freddy's 35th birthday, also become part of Freddy's taxable estate, which is subject to estate tax, and Uncle Sam may be able to claim part of your legacy when Freddy passes away.

On the other hand, if the access side of the teeter-totter stays low, for example if you say something like "and the trustee shall make distributions to Susie Beneficiary only for her health, education and maintenance," you will be pushing down the access side of the teeter-totter somewhat, which will force the protection side of the teeter-totter higher. Susie will have significant protection of the wealth in her trust from creditors, lawsuits, divorce courts, etc. In addition, if the trust is correctly written, the wealth in the trust will not be part of Susie's estate that is subject to estate tax, and her descendants will enjoy the benefits of your legacy without Uncle Sam being able to take away some of the assets when Susie passes away.

But I don't want to exercise excessive control; isn't there some way to provide protection without too much control?

Yes, there is, and some people do not want to establish a high level of control. Luckily for them, a Legacy Plan can be written to provide a very high degree of protection without overly inhibiting the various loved ones' enjoyment of the legacy. With the guidance of a good attorney your can learn how you can balance the teeter-totter just right for each beneficiary.

If a person wants to exercise minimal control over a beneficiary, but provide significant protection for the beneficiary, the plan simply needs to incorporate the appropriate "standards" for distribution of the Legacy to the beneficiary.

What are "standards?"

A "standard" can be any words you include that guide the trustee and tell the trustee when he/she *can* or *must* make distributions. For example, if you tell the trustee that distributions are limited to "health and education," that means the trustee cannot make distributions for any other purpose (such as "maintenance" of a living standard). You might call this the "get a job" standard—and people often prefer this standard for beneficiaries in their 20s, 30s or even 40s.

On the other hand, you could tell the trustee that distributions can be made for "health, education *and maintenance*," and to be liberal with the distributions, which means that the trustee can make distributions to maintain a comfortable standard of living—a very broad and flexible standard. This is often appropriate if the client has small children and wants to ensure that they will be well taken care of up to a certain age. It also is appropriate for many other older beneficiaries. You might call this the "you can retire from your job" standard—and clients often prefer this for young children and beneficiaries in their 50s or 60s.

Do you have to pick only one standard?

No, and that is what makes your Legacy Plan unique. You can pick different standards for different beneficiaries. For example, you may want a fairly liberal standard for a 55-year-old daughter with very good financial sense and very good management skills, and a significantly more conservative standard for a 22-year-old grandchild who may have substance abuse problems.

In addition, you can have shifting standards. For example, you could create a plan where the standard is fairly conservative until the beneficiary reaches a certain age, at which time the instructions shift to fairly liberal standards.

By the way, don't be put off by the labels "conservative" and "liberal" when describing standards. People who are politically liberal often choose conservative distribution standards, whereas many politically conservative people choose liberal distributions standards.

In addition, the variety of standards is endless and the labels "conservative" and "liberal" don't begin to describe the spectrum of choices. Many people turn away from the "typical" standards and write their very own standards for distribution. For example, you could set a fairly conservative standard, but reward certain milestones. For instance, you could provide that the trustee should make a $25,000 gift to the beneficiary upon graduation from college, a $10,000 gift to a beneficiary reaching a ten-year wedding anniversary, and so on.

Is there a minimum standard I must use to provide protection?

The issue is "protection from whom?" If you only want to provide protection from Uncle Sam, using the IRS-approved "health, education and maintenance" standard (or one that is more restrictive) is sufficient to prevent the wealth in the trust to be included in the beneficiary's taxable estate. This means that (assuming the rest of the trust is correctly written) Uncle Sam will not be able to levy estate taxes on the money in the trust when the beneficiary passes away, and the wealth in the trust will pass to the next generation, entirely free of estate taxes.

If you want to provide protection from Uncle Sam, and also provide protection from predators, creditors, lawsuits and divorce, then you again need to use a standard that is at least as restrictive as "health, education and maintenance," and you must also include certain other provisions discussed in the next Chapter.

Finally, if you also want to provide the beneficiary with protection from not only Uncle Sam and other people, but also from the beneficiary's own possible poor judgment or poor management skills, you need to use a carefully crafted standard, more restrictive than "health, education and maintenance" and you need to also employ the provisions discussed in depth in Chapters 5 and 16 of this book.

How do I know which standard to use for my loved ones?

That is the job of your estate planning attorney—he or she will spend most of the first few meetings with you simply listening, and asking quite a few key questions. Once an experienced estate planning attorney gets to know you, your values, your goals and your loved ones, he or she can help you select the appropriate standards for each beneficiary, or can help you craft your own unique standards.

Doesn't this process, crafting unique standards for my beneficiaries, cost a lot of money?

Not necessarily—remember that if you are working with an experienced estate planning attorney, who does this every day, he or she can help you determine the correct standards for your loved ones much more quickly than you can imagine. Of course, a plan will cost slightly more if it is crafted to fit your unique situation, rather than being a one-size-fits-all, fill-in-the-blank form. As any experienced estate planning attorney can tell you, the plans that are the cheapest to put in place often turn out to be the most expensive in the long run: they usually incur probate fees, unnecessary taxes and other expenses. Most important, they bear a huge hidden cost: the wasting of your only opportunity to forge a true and lasting legacy for your loved ones with your hard-earned wealth.

PART II: THE BASIC SOLUTIONS

Chapter 3

- The Revocable Living Trust -

People often get caught up in the debate of "should I have a will or a trust." You can read magazine and newspaper articles, you may hear radio ads, or may get direct mail advertisements filled with information (and misinformation) and various opinions on the need for wills and trusts, and why one is better than the other. The thing you should realize is that both wills and trusts are simply tools, each with a specific use. To debate whether a will or a trust is a better tool is as useless as debating whether a hammer is a better tool than a saw. Which is a better tool depends, of course, on whether you need to drive a nail or cut a board. Usually, if you are building something, both are indispensable. This Chapter will discuss the legal documents you can use to control the distribution of your property when you pass away, which are the estate planners tools. You will learn what a will is and what a revocable living trust is, and how each of them works.

What is a will?

Most people know that a will is the time-honored document by which a person can name the person to take control of his or her property when he or she dies. It also names the people or organizations that a person wants to receive his or her property when he or she dies. In Colorado, the person who you name to take control of the property is called the ***personal representative***; the people who are to receive the property are the ***beneficiaries.***

Here are a few important things to understand about wills: A will gives no one any power to do anything with any of your property as long as you are alive. A will just "sits there silently" with absolutely no effect until the day you die. At your death, if you have a will, your personal representative's power will only become effective after the personal representative gets permission to proceed from a judge. This process of obtaining permission from a judge is called a ***probate proceeding.*** In addition, your personal representative does not have power over everything you own: certain types of property that you own simply are not subject to either the provisions of your will. What types of property are subject to a will, and what types of property are not are discussed later in this Chapter.

What is a trust?

Many people would be surprised to find that trusts are also very time-honored tools to transfer property, with hundreds of years of history. Very simply, a trust is actually a legal arrangement between three people; the ***trustmaker*** (sometimes called the "grantor" or, in old language, the "settlor"), the ***trustee*** and the ***beneficiary.*** A trust is created when a trustmaker turns property over to a trustee, who holds it for a beneficiary.

So, the trustmaker is the person who puts property in

trust by giving it to the trustee. The trustee is the person who holds the property (lawyers call this "having bare, legal, title"). The trustee, however, has a duty to use the property only for the benefit of the trust's beneficiaries, and not for him or herself. The beneficiaries are the people who are entitled to receive the trust property, or the benefits of the trust property (lawyers call this "having beneficial title").

One person alone can play one, two, or all three of these roles. For example: In a situation where a mother or father sets up a bank account for a minor child, the parents are the trustmakers and the trustees, and the child is the beneficiary. In addition, the roles can shift over time. The trustmakers may set the trust up so that they are the initial trustees and beneficiaries, but there will be different trustees when they become incapacitated and different beneficiaries when they die.

What makes a trust a "revocable living trust?"

There is nothing special or mysterious about "revocable living trusts."

A trust is "revocable" if the trustmaker can go to the trustee after he or she has given property to the trustee and take the property back or change the terms upon which the trustee makes distributions to the beneficiaries. (This is in contrast to an "irrevocable" trust, where the trustmaker cannot take the property back or make any changes to the terms of the trust—these types of trusts are set up for special purposes only and are discussed later in this book.)

A "living trust" is any trust that is set up and becomes effective while the trustmaker is alive. The alternative is a testamentary trust, a trust that becomes effective only when the trustmaker dies. A testamentary trust is set up if a person declares in his or her will that he or she wants to leave property in trust for a loved one.

So, a revocable living trust is simply a trust that is set up while the trustmaker is alive, and that allows the trustmaker to take back his or her property at any time, or to make changes to the terms of the trust at any time.

It is very common in the revocable living trusts for the trustmaker to also be the initial trustee and the initial beneficiary of the trust. For example, if you were to set up a revocable living trust you would likely name yourself as the initial trustee of your trust, and you could administer the trust for your sole benefit during your lifetime (with your loved ones becoming the beneficiaries after you die).

What is the difference between a revocable living trust and a will?

The primary difference between a will and a trust in the world of estate planning is that the revocable living trust can solve *two* major challenges: First, it can handle the issue of who will manage and take care of your property if you are mentally incapacitated (disabled). Then, it can also set forth who will take control of your property and make sure that it goes to the people you choose if you pass away. The revocable living trust solves the first problem by naming a successor trustee to replace the initial trustee if the trustmaker becomes mentally incapacitated, and can no longer act as trustee. It solves the second problem because the revocable living trust also controls who will become the successor trustee when the trustmaker dies, and who will then become be the trust's beneficiaries.

It is important to understand, however, that the successor trustees will have control over only the property that is actually owned by the trust. For example, suppose Bill Sample owns a house, but the deed simply shows "Bill Sample" as the owner. Suppose Bill also owns a bank account but the bank account shows "The Bill Sample Trust" as the owner. If Bill becomes mentally incapacitated, whoever Bill has named as successor trustee will be able to take control of the bank account and use the money in the account to take care of Bill. However, because the house is not owned by Bill's trust, the successor trustee will have no ability to do anything with the house. In the same way, when Bill dies, the trustee of Bill's trust will be able to immediately access the money in the bank account and give it to whoever Bill named as his beneficiaries, but the trustee will not be able to administer the house as Bill wished. (Of course a good estate planning attorney would ensure that this does not happen; however, it is important to understand that a trust only controls the property which is actually owned by the trust — if Bill and his attorney had taken the additional step of titling the house into the name of the trust, the trustee could also immediately administer the home as Bill wished, easily and inexpensively.)

A will, on the other hand, is much more limited. In a will, a person declares who he or she wants to take control of her property when he or she dies, and who he or she wants to receive his or her property when he or she dies. The person nominated to take control of the property (the "Personal Representative") has no ability to take control of any property as long as the person who made the will is alive, even if he or she is totally disabled or mentally incapacitated. For example, if Bill Sample prepares a will and names his wife, Mary Sample, as his Personal Representative, and if Bill later became mentally incapacitated, Mary would not be able to access any money in any account owned by Bill or sell any property owned by Bill, even if she needed it for Bill's benefit and care.

Compounding the disability problem, a Personal Representative has no control over property that the deceased person owned as a joint tenant with another person, or property such as life insurance, annuity contracts, IRAs, or 401(k) plans that are not controlled by the provisions of a will. Therefore, one of the shortcomings of a will as an estate planning tool is that it cannot make provisions for a person's disability or mental incapacity.

Finally, when someone does pass away, the Personal Representative must get permission from a District Court Judge in order to be able to take control of the deceased's person's property. The process of getting this permission from a judge is known as the "probate" process. (One major advantage of trust-based planning is that the successor trustee of a revocable living trust does not have to get permission from a judge to deal with any property in the trust.)

In summary, a revocable living trust:

- Allows you to name a person to handle your property if you are mentally incapacitated;
- Allows you to decide who will receive your property when you die, and who will make sure those people receive that property;

- Controls all property that you title in the name of your trust; and

- Does not require the successor trustee to commence any form of probate proceedings or obtain permission from a probate judge in order to manage and administer the trust property.

On the other hand, a will:

- Provides a means for you to name a Personal Representative to control your property when you die and to name the people who should receive the property;

- Only allows the Personal Representative to access your property after you die, not during any period that you are mentally incapacitated;

- Only works with property that you own in your own name alone, not with property you own jointly with another person, or as a contract, or that you own in a revocable living trust; and

- Requires the Personal Representative to get permission from a probate judge in order to deal with your property.

Therefore, both tools have particular uses, and most people need both: a trust as their primary planning instrument, which will avoid probate proceedings and provide for protection in the event of incapacity, and a will to convey any property owned in their own name into the trust.

I have heard that I don't need a trust because probate is simple in Colorado. Is that true?

It is true that Colorado's probate process is less complicated than the probate process in some other States (such as California or Florida), but that does not make it a "simple" process. There are still various legal requirements that must be dealt with, filings with the Court that must be made, and deadlines that must be observed (for a complete discussion of probate proceedings in Colorado see Chapter 14, Probate and Intestacy). Therefore, just because the probate process is less complex in Colorado than it is in some other states, that fact does not necessarily mean that you want your loved ones to deal with inconvenience and expense of a probate proceeding.

If you *want* to minimize the time, inconvenience and expense, of settling your affairs when you die, then what you *need* is to work with an attorney who is committed to providing you the counsel and advice necessary to create a plan that will result in minimized costs for your family. In most cases, because it can avoid the expense of a probate proceeding, as well as provide for management of your property in the event of incapacity, you will choose to use a revocable living trust as your primary planning instrument.

Will I lose control of my property if I put it in a trust?

If the trust is a revocable living trust, the answer is "No." If you are the trustmaker of a revocable living trust, and you name yourself as the initial trustee and beneficiary, then you will retain control of all of your property. In addition, because the trust is "revocable" you have the power to either amend the trust or to have the trustee (you) return all of the trust's property to you at any time.

If I can't be the trustee of my trust anymore, then what happens?

There are only two situations where you will stop acting as the trustee of your revocable living trust: One is if you become mentally incapacitated; the other is if you die. To prepare for both of these situations you will name the successor trustees that you want to take over as the trustee of your trust.

Your next question may be, "Who should I name as my successor trustees?" The choice of trustee to care for your property while you are mentally incapacitated and after you die should be made carefully. Most people immediately consider some family member. The clients reason that family members are familiar with their situation and believe the family members will take on the role of trustee out of love and a sense of duty, and not in order to make money.

However, you should realize that being a trustee is a significant responsibility. The trustee of a trust has a duty to protect the trust property and use it only for the trust's beneficiaries. A trustee must be very careful to keep any trust property totally separate from his or her own property. For example, a trustee cannot move the trust's money into his or her own bank account "because it would be easier to deal with it there." If the trustee did that, it would be difficult, if not impossible, to keep straight how much of the money in the account belonged to the trust, and how much belonged to the trustee. The trustee must keep good records of all property that the trust started with, money paid to the trust, and any expenses paid out of the trust. Therefore, anyone acting as trustee must have an ability to keep good records and be able to prepare a trust tax return.

For these reasons, it may be a good idea to have a professional fiduciary (trust company, CPA, etc.) act as either a trustee or a co-trustee (along with a chosen family member). A professional will, of course, charge a fee for this, although it is usually much less than most people imagine. The most important fact is that the professional trustee will be well prepared to do a complete and thorough job of managing the trust assets. A popular option is to have a family member and a professional trustee serve together. A well drafted trust will allow the family member and professional trustee to divide up the trustee duties. For example, the professional trustee could be responsible for the less convenient aspects of trust administration (keeping the books and records of the trust), and for making the distributions from the trust, whereas the family member could be responsible simply for ongoing supervision and ensuring that you are well cared for.

It is also important to look at the conditions under which a successor trustee could be removed and replaced. Circumstances and conditions change over time, and a person who would be an appropriate trustee today may not be appropriate ten years from now.

Therefore, there are many options in choosing a successor trustee for your revocable living trust. Because this is a critical aspect of your Legacy planning, this is where working with a good, counseling-oriented attorney will provide value for you and your family.

Do we have to file any special tax returns?

As long as you are alive, the trust will use your social security number and any income from property in the trust will simply be reported on your income tax return—in other words, from an income tax standpoint, absolutely nothing changes.

On the other hand, after you die the trust will become irrevocable (this is a good thing – you don't want your wishes to be changed after you die). At that time the trust will to file its own separate tax return, although it is usually a fairly easy return to prepare.

If I set up a revocable living trust how much will a trust company charge to be trustee?

As long as you are alive and not mentally incapacitated and are serving as the trustee of your revocable living trust, the trust company will not be acting as trustee and there is no reason to pay any trustee's fees. If you list a trust company to serve as a successor trustee, it will only begin to collect fees when it begins doing the actual work of being the trustee (i.e. if you become incapacitated or die).

Chapter 4

- Disability Planning and Advance Directives -

What is meant by "disability planning?"

Disability is a broad term. Here we are not talking about all types of disability. For this discussion, the term "disability" refers to either mental incapacity, a mental state where someone cannot handle money or property, such as a person in a coma, or suffering from dementia or Alzheimer's disease, or a physical disability which is so profound that it prevents a person from handling his or her own finances.

If you were to become mentally incapacitated, who would write checks for you, pay your mortgage, or pay your other bills? Who would make medical decisions for you and give instructions to your doctors? Finally, who would have the right to say that you would want certain treatments or, on the other hand, it is time for the doctors to discontinue medical treatment?

In this Chapter we will look at who can make decisions for you if you are incapacitated in each of these three areas: ***Property Decisions, Health Care Decisions, End of Life Decisions.***

1. Property Decisions

Who can take care of my property if I am disabled?

This is a very important question. The question is every bit as important, if not even more important, than the question of who will take control of your property when you die, since this decision could directly impact your quality of life! It is very important to understand that you have to actually take action to put a disability plan into place because there are few "automatics" in these situations. For example, a wife does not automatically have the authority to deal with any property that her husband owns in his own name (such as an IRA, 401-k, cash value life insurance, stocks and bonds or bank accounts).

If you own property in your own name (when no one else is a joint tenant with you) and you have no disability planning, then a Court must become involved and a Judge will appoint who the Judge thinks is best able to manage your property – and this may not be the person that you would choose! Colorado law actually creates two Court-appointed roles: the *conservator* is the Court-appointed person who takes care of someone's property, and the *guardian* is the Court-appointed person who looks after the person's well being and makes health care decisions.

Only a Court can name a conservator or guardian for someone. This process requires filing a petition for conservatorship with the district court in the county where the disabled person is living. The proposed conservator must appear before a judge. The judge may decide to have the Colorado State Division of Social Service examine the disabled person, or may require that the disabled person's doctors testify that the person does not have the mental capacity to handle his or her own affairs.

The judicial process for appointing a conservator is sometimes called "living probate." It can be costly, time consuming, and it is public. For this reason most people, if they realize the difficulty caused by Court involvement, choose to do their own disability planning through powers of attorney and revocable living trusts, which are discussed below.

This process for appointing a conservator does not sound good; can't I just put my spouse's or children's name on my property and let them deal with it if I am mentally incapacitated?

The answer is, "Not necessarily." This practice may cause greater problems, while not being much of a solution.

Generally, if two or more people own something as joint tenants, one joint tenant does not have the ability to deal with the property alone. This tends to be a misunderstood point because so many married couples have joint checking accounts where either husband or wife can sign a check. But in the case of real estate, one joint tenant alone cannot sell, or mortgage the real estate. With brokerage accounts, it usually takes both joint tenants to make withdrawals, close the account or move it to another financial planner. Therefore, joint ownership may work for a few assets, but it will not work for all assets.

Joint ownership can also cause other, unexpected, problems. For example, if one joint tenant is sued, his or her creditor can take all of any jointly owned property to satisfy the debt. For instance, suppose Mary, a single widow, puts her son on the title to her house as a joint tenant to "simplify things." Later, if her son declares bankruptcy or loses a lawsuit, the bankruptcy trustee or the people who filed the lawsuit against her son can take Mary's house to satisfy her son's debts – not her son's "half" of the house, the entire house.

Another problem would be if Mary wants to sell the house, to downsize and have additional money to live on, and her son does not want her to sell. He can stop the sale if he is a joint owner. Finally, owning a home in joint tenancy can cause unnecessary (and significant) income tax problems for Mary's son after Mary dies.

For these reasons (and many more), most estate planners discourage using joint tenancy for disability and estate planning purposes.

What are my other options for having someone take care of my property for me if I am disabled?

Generally, the two best options for allowing someone to take care of your property for you if you become disabled are: powers of attorney and revocable living trusts.

What is a power of attorney for property management?

Many people have heard of powers of attorney. With a power of attorney you can give someone else the authority to conduct business for you. That someone could be a family member, a trusted advisor, or a trust company. The person who gives the power of attorney is known as the "principal."

The person who the principal gives the authority to is known as the "agent." Many people believe that all powers of attorney say the same thing. They do not.

If you want to be sure that your family will have no problems helping you if you are mentally incapacitated, you should understand what works and what does not work in a power of attorney.

When and for how long is a power of attorney effective?

A problem with many powers of attorney is that at common law the power held by the agent ends if the principal becomes mentally incapacitated— even though this defeats the whole point of having a power of attorney! However, you can get around this if the power of attorney is a "durable" power of attorney. A durable power of attorney contains a statement that the power continues even if the principal is mentally incapacitated.

A durable power of attorney can be written as "immediately effective," meaning the agent can go out and conduct business on behalf of the principal as soon as it is signed—most people do not want this for estate planning purposes, they want to remain in complete control while they have their mental capacity. For most people, it is preferable that the power of attorney becomes effective only when the principal becomes mentally incapacitated. This type of power of attorney is often known as a "springing" power of attorney. This is because the agent's power "springs to life" when the principal becomes mentally incapacitated. Although some states do not allow springing powers of attorney, they are specifically allowed in Colorado.

What can someone do with a power of attorney?

A power of attorney must specifically state what things the principal has authorized the agent to do, or not to do. But there is no way to know when you sign a power of attorney what your circumstances will be at the time you become incapacitated. In other words, you don't know what property you will own, what bank you will have an account with, what mutual funds you may own, etc.

This is why many people sign a "general durable" power of attorney as part of their estate planning. A general durable power of attorney is one that describes the agent's power as broadly as possible, and gives the agent authority to do many different transactions. This could include the authority to close savings accounts, cash-in savings bonds, sell stock, or sell real estate. Sometimes general durable powers of attorney include language that says, "My agent may conduct any transaction I could conduct if I were present." You can see from this list that giving someone a general durable power of attorney essentially gives them a "blank check" to deal with your property, which is why it is so important to name the agent carefully.

Who should I name as my agent on a power of attorney?

You can name any individual who is over eighteen, a professional trustee (CPA, etc.), or a trust company. As noted above, most people want to name a family member (or more than one member) as their agent. You should be careful when naming a family member or friend as your agent. The person must be proficient at keeping a checking account, and reconciling that account each month. It is important that anyone acting as the agent for a mentally incapacitated person be very scrupulous in keeping the incapacitated person's money separate from his or her own, not using that person's money for themselves, and being able to account for all income and expenditures.

You might also consider naming a professional fiduciary as an agent on a power of attorney. For example, trust companies will act as agents on powers of attorney, and sometimes CPA's are also willing to take on this role. The benefit of a professional is that they already have the tools in place to manage someone else's assets on their behalf.

Are there times when a power of attorney will not work?

You may have noticed that there is a lot of concern these days about identity theft and people getting into another's accounts without permission. This is why many companies that control your assets (such as banks or brokerage houses) want to be sure that someone who is trying to get information about your accounts, or trying to access your accounts, actually has your permission.

In this environment, it is not unusual that many financial institutions view powers of attorney with suspicion. Also, there is no way for a financial institution to know if a power of attorney has been revoked or not. For these reasons, the financial institutions will only honor a power of attorney if it was signed within the previous twelve months.

For these reasons, most estate planners prefer to use revocable living trusts for effective disability planning (see below) and only use durable powers of attorney for specific purposes. For example, it is a very good idea to have the administrator of your retirement plans from work (401(k), 403(b) plans, etc.) as well as the custodian of your IRAs review your general durable power of attorney. You should find out ahead of time if the plan administrator will take instructions from your agent regarding your retirement plan if you are mentally incapacitated. If they have any issues, objections or reservations, you can ask them for their specific durable power of attorney that your agent can use to manage your retirement assets. A good estate planning attorney is familiar with this important issue and can assist you with dealing with your retirement plan.

Finally, because many financial institutions are hesitant to deal with an agent named in a power of attorney it is a good idea to find out if your financial institution has a time limit for powers of attorney. That is, if it has been more than some period of time since the power was originally signed, will they refuse to honor it? For this reason (and others), it is wise to review your estate planning documents on a regular basis.

How does a revocable living trust work as an alternative to a power of attorney?

When a revocable living trust is created, the trustmaker, trustee, and beneficiary can all be the same person. As we discussed in the last chapter, the trust will have provisions to appoint a new trustee if the original trustmaker ever becomes incapacitated. Therefore, the person you choose as successor trustee will take over management of your property, without Court involvement, and without the problems detailed above, which affect all powers of attorney. You would still be the beneficiary of the trust, and the trust document could say that the trustee can only distribute the trust's assets to you or specific family members or other loved ones (not to themselves).

If the trust is properly drafted, financial institutions holding accounts in the name of a revocable living trust usually will have no problem working with your successor trustee. This is because the account is owned by the trust, and the financial institution *must* deal with the trustee. This is different from a power of attorney, where you own the property and the bank can decide whether or not it wants to work with the person you have named as your agent in the power of attorney.

Moreover, with a revocable trust there can be more flexibility to describe how you want your assets to be used for your care during any time that you are disabled.

This does not mean that trusts are good and powers of attorney are useless. Both are tools that have their purposes. It is important to remember that revocable living trusts only control of property that you have actually titled in the name of the trust. Therefore, every quality estate plan still requires a durable power of attorney which will allow your chosen people to finish transferring assets into the trust if you become incapacitated sooner than expected and which allows them to manage retirement plan assets. A good estate planning attorney can assist you in selecting the right kind of durable powers of attorney to put in place to back up your revocable living trust and achieve total disability planning.

2. Health Care Decisions

Why do I need to say who will make health care decisions for me?

A doctor cannot treat you without your consent; a doctor who treats someone without his or her consent risks being accused of assault. Also, doctors have to be careful to not give your private medical information to someone other than you without your consent. If you became incapacitated, who could give consent for your care and look at your medical records?

If you have nothing in writing about who can make your medical decisions for you upon incapacity, Colorado law provides the answer: when a doctor determines that a person cannot give consent to medical treatment, the doctor must make a reasonable effort to locate as many "interested persons" as possible, and then that group makes "reasonable efforts to reach a consensus as to whom among them shall make medical decisions on behalf of the patient." Who are these "interested persons" under the law? They are the patient's "...spouse, either parent, any adult child, a sibling, a grandchild, or any close friend."

Most people agree that this is not the way that they want their medical decisions to be made.

What if the interested people don't agree, or what if one of the interested persons decides he or she does not like the other interested persons' decision? That person can go to Court and start a guardianship proceeding. This would be like the procedure for naming a conservator discussed in the Property Decisions section.

If you are married you may assume that your spouse will have the right to make medical decisions for you, and that is generally true. But without something in writing declaring that your spouse is the one you wish to make the decisions, a child or a friend has the right to go to court and hold everything up while a judge makes the decision. Moreover, maybe you don't want your spouse to make those decisions. Many couples want an older child to make such medical decisions, worrying that the stress of making such decisions might be too stressful for their spouse at such an already stressful time.

How do I avoid what you just described?

The way to avoid having the problem described above is to name someone *of your choice* as your *agent for making health care decisions* (also known as proxy health care decision maker, health care agent, etc.). The document for doing this is a power of attorney for health care decisions.

After seeing what Colorado law requires when no one is named as agent for health care decisions, it is not surprising that hospitals want a copy of your power of attorney for health care whenever you are admitted. If a patient cannot produce a health care power of attorney, the hospital will ask the patient to complete a health care power of attorney form provided by the hospital before he or she is admitted—they don't want the mob scene in the hall required by Colorado law if a power of attorney for health care decisions is not in place. However, this effort on the part of the hospital does not address the issue of what to do if you are admitted when you can no longer complete a power of attorney designation. That is why you must do it in advance.

Are there any guidelines for whom I should name as my agent?

Here are two guidelines worth considering:

First, name only one person to be your agent for making health care decisions. Some people want to name groups of people to be the decision maker. However, doctors say it is much better of the doctors know specifically who he or she will talk to and who they must take orders from. If you name a group (such as "all of my children") and they cannot agree, then the process slows down, and there is still the possibility that a Court will be asked to make the decision.

Some people want to name all of their children so that no child is left feeling that her mother or father preferred one of the children. This could be remedied by writing a letter to your children explaining why you chose one child to act alone, and suggesting that that child consult with all other children before making any decisions.

Second, always name a back up person, or two, or three (also known as "successors"). The back up people would have the power to act if the first person you named was not able to act for any reason.

3. End of Life Decisions

What is a living will?

An advance care directive (often called a "living will") is a document by which you specify whether or not you want certain medical treatments and what sort of treatment you want. Suppose that the day came that it was clear that you are dying, and the opinion of your doctors is that it is only a matter of time (weeks, days, or hours) before you die, and that any treatment will only prolong the inevitable. At what point would you want to say, "Stop, enough, no more treatment, let me go?" The living will is the way that you can tell your agents and doctors how you feel about this issue and allows you to give them specific instructions.

The follow up question is: what if you can't say what you want at that point in time? What if you are unconscious— what happens then? At that point, will the doctors follow the instructions of your family, or will the doctors be in control? Many people are troubled by the thought that a doctor may not follow their family's wishes.

Now that medical techniques allow doctors to keep people alive to an extent that was unknown fifty or one hundred years ago, we are all aware of these questions and issues. In response to these developments, and to some high-profile cases (Karen Anne Quinlan, Nancy Cruzan and Terry Schiavo), the courts and legislatures of the various states have attempted to set guidelines to answer these questions.

Generally, each of the states has passed a law that allows you to make known ahead of time your wishes about discontinuing medical treatment. You do this by means of a living will (also called advanced medical directive), which is a statement of your desire regarding the termination of medical treatment if you ever are in a position where you cannot communicate.

Many people feel strongly that they want to minimize the financial and emotional burden of watching doctors expend heroic efforts when death is inevitable. If you have those feelings, here are some things to consider.

Does a living will mean that someone can let me die even if there is a chance I will get better?

Absolutely not! There is some confusion around the term "pull the plug," and many people believe that a living will is a statement of, "If my condition gets to a certain point, then go ahead and kill me." This is not a living will; a living will is not a euthanasia declaration. Euthanasia is not legal in Colorado. What living wills attempt to do is make clear the specific conditions when you would want to say, "stop the medical treatment and let me go" if you were able to speak.

Do I need a living will if my family knows what I want?

You may think that your family knows your wishes, but they probably don't—or in any event, would like to have your wishes written down so that they can be sure how you feel when the time comes for them to make a difficult decision. Don't forget that the Terry Schiavo case was about whether to believe the family member who said Terry would want the treatment stopped, or whether to believe the family members who said she would want it continued.

Each state has its own unique laws regarding living wills. Colorado law requires that the signing of the living will be witnessed by two people who are totally uninterested in your finances and health care.

In addition to a living will, you should sign a health care power of attorney as discussed above. In a health care power of attorney you name an agent to make health care decisions for you, including the powers to put your wishes into effect. Of course, a health care power of attorney covers more situations than just discontinuing medical treatment, so you should read the health care power of attorney to be sure that it allows your agent to discontinue medical treatment, if that is your wish. You could also write a letter to your health care agent giving them specific directions as to how you want to be treated in different situations.

What was unique about the Terry Schiavo case?

Terry Schiavo didn't actually need medical treatment to stay alive. She lived for many years in a "persistent vegetative state." She stayed alive through artificially provided nutrition and hydration, and whether to discontinue that nutrition was the issue that her family disagreed upon.

If you feel strongly about end of life decisions, it is a good idea to make clear your desire to have nutrition and hydration continued or discontinued if you should end up in a persistent vegetative state.

Our Colorado living will law addresses this issue: It allows someone to state that if "the only procedure being provided is artificial nourishment," then either: (1)

Discontinue artificial nourishment, (2) Continue artificial nourishment for a declared number of days, or (3) Continue artificial nourishment indefinitely.

It would also be wise to have a statement in your health care power of attorney giving your health care agent the power to either continue or discontinue hydration and nourishment if you are in a persistent vegetative state.

How do I make sure that someone can find my living will if I am in a coma?

If you prepare and sign a living will or health care power of attorney, and no one can find it when the time comes, it will do you absolutely no good. It is a good idea to give copies to your health care provider. There are also services that will keep copies of your living will and health care power of attorney on file and provide them to medical providers when they are needed.

Chapter 5

- Your Loved Ones' Inheritance: Protected Indefinitely -

What is "asset protection?"

Asset protection is a big topic, it would take a whole, separate, book to provide a complete overview of asset protection. In this book, we will look at just a few asset protection issues.

This Chapter is about how you can protect what you leave to your loved ones from their future potential creditors, lawsuits, or failed marriages. Chapter 9 will discuss techniques you may wish to employ to protect *your* assets from *your* creditors.

Is any of my property in a revocable living trust protected from creditors?

This is a common misconception. If you set up a revocable living trust (you are the trustmaker, beneficiary, and trustee and reserve the right to revoke the trust), you have total control and access to your trust assets, so your creditors can "step into your shoes" to get at anything in that trust. The trust provides no asset protection.

Why would I want to protect what I am going to leave my loved ones from creditors?

You should consider that people are living longer and, with each passing year, we live in a world that is subject to rapid, ongoing change and uncertainties. You may have had the opportunity to work for one employer for many years and to receive a pension or to build up a substantial retirement account. In our current economic world, your children may never have those same opportunities. Your children's inheritance may be a critical part of their retirement.

We do not know what will happen in the future. How long will your children live after you are gone, and what sorts of things will happen to them? It is impossible to predict if they will be hit with a frivolous lawsuit or end up getting divorced.

How could my children lose their inheritance in a divorce?

When a couple divorces in Colorado, each keeps his or her separate property and divides any marital property "equitably" (usually fifty-fifty). Separate property is any property that someone owned before getting married and any property received during the marriage by a gift or through inheritance. Marital property includes the increase in value for any separate property that occurs during the marriage and any property acquired by both during the marriage.

It is not unusual for someone to receive an inheritance and then put it into jointly owned property. This could happen by paying off the mortgage on the family house (most married couples own their homes as joint tenants), or by placing it in a jointly owned brokerage account. As soon as a child puts his or her inheritance into jointly owned property with his or her spouse, it becomes marital property. If that child later gets divorced, he or she will lose one half of her inheritance. Even if a child keeps his or her inheritance separate, the increase in value of that inheritance can be considered to be marital property.

The best way to assure that the inheritance does not become marital property is to leave it to a child in a trust that lasts for the child's whole life. We call this a Lifetime Protective Trust.

When I had a will prepared I told the attorney that I wanted to be sure that my money went to my grandchildren after my children; how can I be sure this will happen?

You need to be very careful in this case. Most wills and living trusts say that if a child is not alive when the person who made the will dies, then the property set aside for that child then goes to that child's children (the grandchildren). But people (including many attorneys) have not stopped and considered that the more likely chain of events is that the child will receive the inheritance and then die sometime later. If this happens, the child could leave the property to his or her spouse, and his or her spouse can then leave it to whomever he or she wants to upon his or her death. And that means the grandchildren may never ever see the inheritance. This happens much more often than you imagine.

The only way to ensure that any property you leave your children will go to your grandchildren is to leave it to your children in a Lifetime Protective Trust.

Are there any reasons why I would want to leave property to my spouse in a Lifetime Protective Trust?

For a surviving spouse there is the possibility of being sued and having to pay off a creditor, and a protective trust will protect the property in the trust. An additional, often overlooked, issue with many married couples is how to ensure that, if the surviving spouse remarries, the property of the deceased spouse will go to the children of that marriage, and not to the children of some other family. You can accomplish this by leaving property in a protective trust for your spouse.

You should proceed with caution in creating a trust for a spouse. Generally, you can leave an unlimited amount to your spouse when you die, without any federal estate tax liability. Trusts for surviving spouses that qualify for this "no federal estate tax" treatment are called "marital deduction trusts" or "QTIP trusts" (Qualified Terminable Interest Property), and must be set up correctly. You can find out more about marital deduction trusts in Chapter 13.

How do I go about leaving property to my loved ones in a Lifetime Protective Trust?

You should understand that this can be done with either a revocable living trust or a will. The revocable living trust would simply become a trust for your spouse and/or children after your death. Your will can also direct that property be left to a beneficiary in a trust; these are usually called "testamentary trusts" (although you should recall that using a will may subject your family to an unnecessary probate proceeding, see Chapters 3 and 14).

An important consideration in leaving property to your family in trust is making sure that your assets will go to that trust when you die. The only property that will go into a testamentary trust is any property controlled by your personal representative named in your will. This would **not** include property you own with another as a joint tenant, or anything that has a beneficiary designation (like life insurance, annuity contracts, or IRAs). Similarly, a trust created by your revocable trust will only include property that was owned by the trust when you died, or that is directed to the trust on your death either through your pour over will or because the trust is named as the beneficiary of an asset where you are able to name beneficiaries.[1]

Now, you may be asking yourself, "If I leave my property to my spouse or children in a protective trust, doesn't that mean they will have a hard time getting to it? The answer is, "No."

Will my spouse or children lose control of their inheritance if I leave it to them in a Lifetime Protective Trust?

You may be asking why someone would want to limit their children's control over their inheritance. There are some obvious family situations, such as minor children or children with disabilities, where there is a need to have a third party protect and manage your children's inheritance. But the natural concern when the children are normal, successful, adults is that leaving property in trust would mean severely limiting their control.

Traditionally, to take care of the situation where there are minor children, people will have their will or revocable

---

1   Because of potential negative income tax results, you should only name a trust as the beneficiary of a retirement plan account (IRA or 401(k)), or annuity contract after consulting with a professional who is prepared to address the income tax issues associated with having a trust as a beneficiary of any tax-qualified account.

living trust create a trust for their children to hold any property until the children become adults, or complete their education. Another approach is to create a trust for children that will, for example, give them control over one-third of the trust when the child is 30, another third at 35, and the final third at 40. In these situations, the trust ends at some point during the trust beneficiary's life, the trust property is given to the beneficiary, and the beneficiary has total control over the property.

However, the shortcoming of this approach is that once the beneficiary has total control over the property, it is exposed to the potential claims of creditors or division in a divorce.

The traditional response to this shortcoming is the possibility of leaving property in a trust with a neutral trustee (such as a bank) who follows your guidelines as to when a beneficiary receives distributions. The trust could also include what is known as a "spendthrift" provision, prohibiting the trustee from making distributions to a beneficiary's creditors and not allowing a beneficiary to pledge or encumber any of the trust property. In this situation it would be very difficult for a creditor to have any access to the trust property. In this situation, the beneficiary would never have any control.

In the last few years some "hybrid" approaches to trusts have developed that are more appropriate in most cases. The goal has been to create lifetime protective trusts with flexibility to meet changing circumstances and changing laws. Some of the solutions include allowing the beneficiary to remove a trustee and appoint a different trustee, or allowing the beneficiary to be the trustee, or to serve as a co-trustee with a trust company or CPA that the beneficiary can choose.

Recently, a trend has developed to draft trusts that distinguish three trustee functions, administration, distribution, and investment. The administrative trustee performs administrative tasks, such as keeping the checkbook and preparing and filing income tax returns. The distributive trustee decides when, to whom, and how much, to distribute from the trust. The investment trustee decides how to invest the trust assets.

In the above scenario, you could have a trust where the beneficiaries could be the investment trustee (the beneficiaries have control over how the trust is invested), a trust company or other neutral trustee could be the distributive trustee, with the beneficiaries having authority to fire the trustee and hire a new one if the trustee is too restrictive in making distributions (the beneficiaries have some control), and a beneficiary could be the administrative trustee (the beneficiary has control over record keeping and tax filings). In this example, if the beneficiary has an issue with a creditor, a judge will have to order the trust company (not the beneficiary) to make a distribution, and the trust company will be able to successfully argue that it cannot make the distribution to the creditor.

Therefore, there are ways to build flexibility into a Lifetime Protective Trust for your loved ones. If you would like to include such trust in your estate plan, it is wise to work with an attorney who understands all of the options available in establishing a Lifetime Protective Trust, who can counsel you as to which options are the most appropriate for your family, and who can build flexibility into your individual plan.

PART III: SPECIAL SITUATIONS

Chapter 6

- Blended Families and Second Marriages -

I'm in a second marriage. Are there any estate planning concerns that are unique to my situation?

There is considerable potential for conflict and resentment in planning for blended families. The conflict arises out of the client's desire to provide for the current spouse, but not disinherit their children from their prior marriage. This can create problems if the available estate planning techniques are not understood or are not properly implemented.

One common goal is to provide sufficient access to property and income for the surviving spouse, so that he or she may continue to live comfortably if his or her spouse were to pass away. An open and frank discussion of the potential for friction and conflict between the surviving spouse and the children from the deceased spouse's first marriage will need to occur. The emotional needs of all those involved will need to be anticipated and considered.

The typical plan utilized for people who have had only one marriage (where at the death of the first spouse all of the property passes to or is held for the use and benefit of the surviving spouse, and at the surviving spouse's death the property passes to the children) will not normally be satisfactory in blended family and second-marriage situations. In these situations the inheritance of the decedent's children could be dependent upon the surviving spouse's spending habits. The decedent's children may view every expenditure of the surviving spouse, and this scrutiny can create conflict and foster resentment. The children may believe that the surviving spouse is living too extravagantly, is taking too many luxurious vacations, or is squandering their prospective inheritance. The surviving spouse, on the other hand, may feel that he or she has not been treated properly by the decedent's children and may retaliate in a manner that would reduce or eliminate the children's inheritance altogether. Ideally, we would like to provide for the surviving spouse and provide for the decedent's children entirely separately. As a consequence, it makes sense to segregate the children's inheritance from the surviving spouse's inheritance.

Should I leave my estate to my spouse or to my children?

Most people want to benefit their spouse in a blended family or second marriage situation and still provide for their children. Experience teaches that the potential for conflict is so great that to follow traditional estate planning patterns could be a mistake that could create problems, legal fees and conflicts between the surviving spouse and the decedent's children.

If the size of the estate is sufficient to divide between the surviving spouse and the decedent's children, the choice is easy. In that case, the decedent's estate is divided and the surviving spouse receives an amount necessary to maintain his or her lifestyle. The children are given their inheritance in the form of a trust or outright distribution that is not dependent upon the actions, lifestyle or spending habits of the surviving spouse.

If the size of the estate is not adequate to take care of both, how do I take care of my spouse without disinheriting my children?

There are several techniques that may be employed if the size of the decedent's estate is not adequate to fully provide for the surviving spouse and fully provide for the decedent's children.

The first technique is to establish a trust for the benefit of the surviving spouse that requires that all of the income of the trust be distributed to the surviving spouse. Income, for purposes of determining the amount to be distributed, is limited to interest, dividends, rents and royalties. Realized capital gain may be included in the definition of income if the trust document specifically expands the definition of income to include realized capital gain. The caution here is that income, regardless of the definition, may not be adequate to support the surviving spouse.

The trust may be designed to prohibit principal distributions to the surviving spouse. The trust may also be designed to permit principal distributions for the surviving spouse's truly necessary health, education and the maintenance needs during the surviving spouse's lifetime. The trust could also be designed to allow the trustee of the trust wide latitude to determine how much, if any, of the principal of the trust to distribute to the surviving spouse (obviously, in such cases neither the surviving spouse nor the children should be designated as trustee). In designing the provisions of the trust that control principal distributions, both the current needs and the future probable needs of the surviving spouse should be considered.

Upon the surviving spouse's death, the remaining balance of the trust passes to the decedent's children. The design considerations for this portion of the trust are the same as those discussed in Chapter 16 on Dynasty Trusts.

The conflicts possible using this first technique, while somewhat diminished, remain substantial. A potential for conflict still remains as to the amounts to be distributed to the surviving spouse. If income distributions are required, there is still a potential conflict between the surviving spouse and the decedent's children. That conflict pertains to how the money in the trust is invested. Does the trustee maximize the income to be generated to the surviving spouse by investing in bonds, CDs, and money market accounts? Or does the trustee maximize the growth of the funds in the trust by investing in stock, real estate and other investments that do not generate much income. The surviving spouse will typically want the trustee to maximize the income generated by the trust and the decedent's children typically will want the trustee to maximize the growth of the trust.

A second technique, which has arisen due to the problems inherent in an "income" trust may provide some relief for this potential conflict. It is called a "total return trust." The trust is designed to provide that a set percentage of the value of the trust is distributed each year to the surviving spouse. The particular percentage to be set forth in the trust will depend on the current and probable future needs of the surviving spouse and the value of the trust. The use of the percentage eliminates the conflict between the surviving spouse and the decedent's children. The trustee is free to invest the trust assets for maximum return on investment. The distinction between income and growth is irrelevant. The surviving spouse wants the trustee to maximize the value of the trust because it increases the amount required to be distributed to the surviving spouse. The decedent's children also want the trustee to grow the value of the trust to maximize the value that will be distributed to them at the death of the surviving spouse. Accordingly, the surviving spouse and the decedent's children have the same goals and disharmony is minimized.

If the client is insurable, a third approach may utilize an irrevocable life insurance trust.[2] The life insurance trust is established for the benefit of the decedent's children. The trust purchases and is named as the beneficiary of the life insurance. The amount of life insurance to be purchased will depend on a number of factors, including the cost of the insurance, the value of the insured's estate, and the amount passing from the insured to the surviving spouse. At the insured's death, the life insurance would pay the death benefit to the irrevocable life insurance trust, which would be held or distributed for the benefit of the decedent's children

---

2   See Chapter 17, Irrevocable Life Insurance Trusts, for more information.

as the decedent intended. The decedent's entire remaining estate (or some portion of that estate) could then pass to the surviving spouse. Monetarily, it could be arranged so that the surviving spouse and the decedent's children could each receive the same amount. This can serve to equalize the parties' interests in the decedent's estate. However, if the children have emotional attachment to the decedent's assets (such as a family farm, the home, or a small business) then, as an alternative, the life insurance trust could be established for the benefit of the surviving spouse and the decedent's children could receive the decedent's other assets.

A qualified estate planning attorney can counsel you on how best to use an irrevocable life insurance trust to solve these planning challenges.

Who should be the trustee of the trust for my surviving spouse?

A common mistake is naming a child as the trustee of a trust that is for the benefit of the surviving spouse. The potential for conflict is aggravated by placing the contingent beneficiary, the child, in control of the administration and distribution of trust income and principal to a surviving spouse. This situation will generally lead to resentment if not outright litigation between the parties. The decedent's children should never be trustees of a trust that is for the benefit of the surviving spouse (similarly, and for the same reasons, the surviving spouse should also not be the trustee). A third-party or professional trustee should be employed to manage the trust assets for the benefit of the surviving spouse and the decedent's children.

Will stepchildren share in the inheritance?

Children, step or otherwise, have no right or claim to assets of a deceased parent or step-parent who has an estate plan. However, if a parent dies without an estate plan, some or all of that parent's assets will pass under Colorado law to their children. Step-children, unless they have been legally adopted, and no matter how close they actually are, are not considered to be descendants of the parent and are not included in the distribution scheme enacted by the Colorado legislature. As a consequence, step-children do not share in the inheritance unless a parent specifically provides for them in a trust or will. The same goes for daughters and sons in law.

How do I prevent my surviving spouse from accessing funds on behalf of his or her children?

The best way to address this concern during the lifetime of the surviving spouse is to provide that the sole and exclusive beneficiary of the trust set up by the decedent shall be only the surviving spouse during his or her lifetime. It is also recommended that the decedent name an independent trustee to administer the trust during the surviving spouse's lifetime, to ensure that these provisions are honored.

Chapter 7

- Estate Planning for Single People -

If you are single, you have all of the same concerns married couples have, plus a few extra, which make it even more critical for you to put a solid estate plan in place. Therefore, while the rest of this book remains fully relevant to you, you should pay attention to certain additional issues.

By "single," estate planners mean anyone who is not legally married, either by choice, divorce, death of a spouse or, in some cases because you are in a non-traditional relationship.

Are there estate tax advantages, or disadvantages, to being single?

No, not really. A married couple has the opportunity to shield two exemption amounts from estate taxes (see Chapter 13, Taxes), and a single person has only the opportunity to shield one exemption amount. This isn't really an advantage or disadvantage, it is just a reflection of the fact that each person has the opportunity to shield one exemption amount from estate taxes, and in a married couple there are two persons.

If you are in a non-traditional relationship, and your combined assets exceed the exemption amount, you may want to employ an estate plan similar to one employed by a prosperous married couple, using a "bypass" trust, as detailed in Chapter 13. This will avoid all of the combined assets being subject to estate tax in the survivor's estate upon the death of the survivor of you.

What is different about estate planning for single people?

The biggest difference is the critical importance of putting a solid disability plan in place. If someone in a marriage becomes disabled, in many cases the doctors, hospitals, banks, brokerage houses, etc., would honor the wishes and direction of a spouse, even if not legally required to do so. If you are single, you simply don't have that "default" decision maker, and you need to put your choice of decision makers firmly in place, and you need to establish their authority in binding legal documents.

For example, if you had no estate plan in place and suffered a stroke, were significantly disabled for a time, and could not communicate your wishes regarding who would manage your property, pay your bills, and take care of you financially, the Court would appoint a conservator to take care of these things for you. Of course, the Court would pick someone they think would do a good job, maybe a parent, sibling, child or professional fiduciary. However, the person that the Court would pick might not be the person you would choose. In other words, you would give up control. For example, suppose that you would want your brother, sister or partner to be your disability trustee—the Court will not know that, and might choose your father or mother, which could be a terrible choice in some families. Estate planning is all about establishing control, and this is definitely an area where you want to establish firm control.

It is even more important to choose your health care agent and establish your chosen agent's authority in your planning documents. Chapters 3 and 4 discussed this in greater depth, but it is important to understand that is absolutely critical for a single person to name the specific person that you want to make your health care decisions for you. Again, if you do not, the Court will name the decision maker, or even worse, the doctors and the hospital may decide who they are going to listen to and whose directions they are going to follow (see Chapter 4, Disability Planning and Advance Directives). For health care decisions, including end of life decisions, you want to ensure that someone who understands your wishes and will honor your wishes is placed firmly in control. If the person you would choose is not a blood relative, then it is even more imperative that you put a plan into place which establishes that person as your decision maker—otherwise that person may be completely ignored by a relative or the relatives who take over your health care.

I'm divorced and my ex and I disagree on everything, especially when it comes to the kids. Can I do an estate plan without my ex-spouse's cooperation?

Yes, in fact, you absolutely must put a good estate plan in place. If you do not, under the laws of intestacy in Colorado, your property will go to your children. That is probably OK with you, except that if the children are minors, there is a good chance that the Court will appoint your ex-spouse (the other parent of the children) as conservator of the children's inheritance. In other words, it is likely that your ex-spouse would end up with control over all of your wealth—which is probably the last thing that you would want! In addition, even if your ex-spouse behaved and administered the property responsibly, he or she would have to turn the property over to your child when your child reaches the age of 21, which is probably the worst time to give someone a large sum of money.

What you would probably want to do instead is name someone who you really trust (or a trust company) as the trustee of the children's inheritance, to administer it for their benefit until they reach an age of maturity and distribution that you are comfortable with.

Your wealth is yours to distribute as you wish. It is always beneficial when divorced parents agree on planning for the children, in which case they can coordinate their estate planning. However, if you don't get along, it is even more important to put your own individual estate plan in place, reflecting your values and wishes for your loved ones, and placing those people who you trust in charge of implementing your wishes.

I'm single with no children, why should I bother to create an estate plan?

First, you need an estate plan to take care of you if you are disabled, as noted above. But beyond that, do you really not care at all what happens to your hard-earned wealth? If you have no plan, the laws of intestacy will control the distribution of your wealth, and your heirs will need to commence a time-consuming probate proceeding to administer your wealth. Rather than simply having various relatives inherit your wealth because that is what the legislature said should happen, wouldn't you really rather that your loved ones know that you cared for them and wanted them to have your hard-earned property? Suppose your only brother was your heir under the laws of intestacy, and you wouldn't alter that with your estate plan—you would leave all of your property to him outright. Wouldn't it be better that he knows that you intentionally left him the property because you cared for him and wanted him to receive your wealth without the inconvenience and expense of a probate proceeding, rather than simply "getting" your wealth in a fairly inconvenient manner because you had no plan? In addition, if you put a plan into place, you can also determine what would happen to your wealth if your brother died before you did.

Finally, many single people without children want their wealth to be used in a meaningful manner. Perhaps as a safety net for a partner, good friend, nieces, nephews, other relatives or other loved ones. Perhaps as an educational fund for relatives or as a gift to a college or scholarship fund. Many clients make gifts to their church or favorite charities.

If you really and truly don't care what happens to your wealth when you pass away, you only need a disability plan; you don't need a will, trust or other wealth distribution estate planning instrument. But do you really not care at all?

Can't I just put my daughter (or son, brother or mother) on my property as a joint tenant?

Estate planning attorneys really do not like to use joint tenancy for planning, because the client completely gives up control over that asset. For example, with joint tenancy:

• If the joint tenant is in an automobile accident and the other driver wins a lawsuit judgment in excess of the available insurance, you could lose your property to the other driver since your joint tenant is deemed to own 100% of the joint tenancy property, even while you are still alive and even if you are entirely blameless (this does happen);

• If the joint tenant has to file bankruptcy, you could lose all (not half) of your property to the bankruptcy trustee (this also happens);

• If your joint tenant becomes disabled and needs to qualify for Medicaid or Supplemental Security Income, the joint tenancy assets will disqualify them from qualifying for these benefits, and you might be required to spend down "their" half of your joint tenancy property on their care before they would qualify for public benefits;

• You gave up total control—suppose the joint tenant survives you by a couple of weeks and then dies. Your property will be administered under that person's estate plan, going to their chosen heirs, not yours.

• It's a one-way street: you can put someone's name on your property as a joint tenant without their knowledge or permission (although you should never do this), but you can't take their name off without their permission. In other words, if you want to sell your home, you will need to get your joint tenant's permission and signature, and they would have the right to demand half of the sale proceeds.

Now you know why estate planning attorneys discourage the use of joint tenancy in almost all planning situations—it is because joint tenancy causes our clients to lose control, and our job is to help our clients establish control. These are just a few of the problems with joint tenancy. In addition, in some situations, using joint tenancy to pass your assets to your loved ones can even lead to increased taxation for the loved ones – just the opposite of what you wanted to accomplish. There are lots of good alternatives to using joint tenancy for your estate planning set forth in this book, and you can discuss which of them is most appropriate in your situation with your attorney.

Chapter 8

- Planning for Loved Ones with Special Needs -

Some families face an additional planning challenge because a loved one has some form of disability and will require some level of extra care or support for life. In some cases this may be a brother, sister, mother or father. In many cases, it is a child. When a member of a family has these additional needs, he or she needs special planning.

What is "special needs" planning?

Special needs planning is highly individualized because the range of special needs is so broad. One family may have a child with a significant but not crippling developmental delay: the child can live independently and will eventually be able to be gainfully employed, although probably at a lower wage. In this case, the parents will want to ensure that the legacy for that child is well managed by a professional for the entire life of that child, that there will be a support and advice network in place, and that the support network and estate plan are set up to encourage maximum independence for that child.

Another family may have a child who is significantly disabled, perhaps with both profound physical and mental disabilities. In that case, the parents will need to ensure that the legacy they leave for that child will provide quality support and care and provide both strong financial and strong guardianship protections for the child's entire life. An additional challenge for this family is how to leave a significant legacy to the disabled child, without that legacy disqualifying that child for needed public health and educational benefits.

In between these two examples there are many other types of special needs plans, e.g., the child with a significant substance-abuse problem, the child with severe emotional difficulties that interfere with employment, and so on.

Special needs planning is the process of setting up a system, or network, that will ensure that the care and support being provided by the parents or other loved ones will continue when the parents or other loved ones become disabled or pass away. Because each child, each family, and each situation is so unique, special needs planning is very different for each family. There are, however, some common issues every family with a special need must address.

I have heard of "Special Needs Trusts." What are they?

A special needs trust is one tool that is used in special needs planning. However, it is important to remember that it is just one tool, just one component, of a good special needs plan—it is not a special needs plan in itself.

A special needs trust is simply an arrangement where a trust holds legal title to various property and where that trust dictates that the property must be used exclusively for the benefit of the special needs beneficiary. The trustee of the trust is given complete discretion on how to use the property in the trust for the benefit of the beneficiary. If it is set up correctly, the beneficiary of the trust (the disabled person) has no ownership or control rights over the trust—this is very important. Because the beneficiary has no ownership of the trust, the property in the trust will not disqualify the beneficiary from any public programs. This is critical because the two major programs that benefit the disabled, Medicaid and Supplemental Security Income ("SSI"), have strict rules that would disqualify a beneficiary if the beneficiary "owns" any significant assets. The key to a successful special needs plan is to create a trust that can hold significant amounts of property, allow the beneficiary to qualify for all public programs, and yet the trustee is empowered and directed to use the property in the trust to supplement those public programs. If done correctly, this sort of plan can greatly enhance the quality of the beneficiary's life.

How would I set up a Special Needs Trust?

Due to the stringent rules of Medicaid and SSI, the actual language of a special needs trust is quite complex. However, the concept is straightforward: the chosen property is placed in trust, with trust administration rules that conform to the various government regulations, and with a competent trustee managing and disbursing the money as needed.

You can create a special needs trust in two ways: as a "testamentary trust" or as a "stand-alone" trust.

A stand-alone trust is just what its name implies: it is a separate document from your will or living trust. The trust comes into being as a legal entity the moment you sign the trust document. From the moment of signing, the trust can own just about anything you can own: a bank account, an investment account, real estate (houses, condominiums, vacant land, etc.), stocks, bonds, etc. If set up properly, it can even be the beneficiary of another person's IRA. For example, Grandpa can name the trust as the beneficiary of his IRA, so that when he passes away, the trust "inherits" the IRA and the trustee allows most of the money to grow tax deferred, but uses the distributions from the IRA for the benefit of the disabled beneficiary of the trust. This is actually a very good planning technique as it allows Grandpa's legacy to the beneficiary to grow tax deferred for a very long time; but this type of planning must be done very carefully to avoid tax problems.

People create stand-alone trusts primarily because they want to have a legal entity in place to hold money or other property, either right now or in the near future. For example, Grandma or Grandpa, or a favorite uncle or aunt may have indicated that they want to leave some money to the disabled child in their estate plan, but are aware that this could cause the child to become ineligible for public benefits, which are an important part of the child's current care network. In this case, the family would want to create a stand-alone trust for the child's benefit, perhaps naming the parents as the current trustees. The generous relative then simply makes the bequest in his or her estate plan to the special needs trust rather than directly to the beneficiary. Upon the relative's death, the money will flow directly into the stand alone special needs trust for the child's benefit, without in any way interfering with the child's eligibility for public benefits.

Are there any other advantages of stand-alone special needs trusts?

There are lots of ways a stand-alone trust can provide significant benefits to a family with a special needs child. For example, in a divorce situation where the husband and wife do not fully trust each other, but want to make some provisions for a special needs child, they might set up a stand-alone trust with a neutral trustee (a trust company that specializes in special needs trusts) administering the donated property for the benefit of the child. This often is the solution for grandparents who are distressed by the divorce and want to make provisions for the grandchild, but do not fully trust either parent to administer the trust prudently.

Another advantage of a correctly formed special needs trust is that, if the correct provisions are included in the trust document, the property in the trust will not be included in the taxable estate of the parents. For example, suppose a mother and father set up a stand-alone special needs trust and the grandfather leaves the trust $50,000 in his will, which is paid directly into the trust upon the grandfather's passing. The trustee of the trust can then take $40,000 of that money and purchase a single-premium insurance policy on the life of the mother or father of the child. Depending upon the age and health of the mother or father, the death benefit could be as high as $500,000, $1,000,000, or even more, which would be used to take care of the disabled child after the parents pass away. Besides the obvious advantage of leveraging up the size of the gift from the grandfather, this money, even if it is millions of dollars, will not be included in the insured parent's estate when he or she dies, producing huge tax savings for his or her estate, and huge tax-free benefits for the disabled child.

If a family has sufficient resources, they can do the same with their own $50,000 (or whatever amount), thereby passing a large legacy to a disabled child inside a special needs trust. In other words, sometimes the money might come from Grandpa, sometimes from mother or father; it doesn't matter. If the money is passed into a correctly formed special needs trust, it will not be included in anyone's taxable estate.

What are the advantages of the other type of trust, the testamentary special needs trust?

A "testamentary" special needs trust is simply one that is set up by the parent's will or revocable living trust—in other words, it does not come into effect as a legal entity until the death of the parent. From that point on, it will stand alone as a trust and function just like a stand-alone special needs trust. In either case, the trust language is the same and the trust will function the same once it comes into being—the difference being that a stand-alone trust comes into being as a legal entity immediately upon signing, while the testamentary trust comes into being as a legal entity upon the death of the person creating the trust.

The two advantages of the testamentary special needs trust are the simplicity during your life and the ability to change the trust. The simplicity comes from the fact that the trust does not legally come into being until your death, so you do not need to open separate bank accounts, file separate tax returns, etc., during your lifetime. In other words, because it does not come into effect until you die, you do not have to administer it during your lifetime. The other advantage is that you can easily change the terms of the testamentary trust, simply by making an amendment to your trust or codicil to your will the same way you would make any other change.

Does this mean that a stand-alone trust cannot be amended?

It depends on the terms of the trust. You can reserve the right to amend the terms of a stand-alone trust if you like, but if you retain that particular right all of the property in the trust will be included in your taxable estate upon your death. Depending on the size of your estate, this may not matter at all, or it can be a very large concern. If you want the property in the trust to be outside of your taxable estate, you need to give the amendment rights to a very trusted third person not related to you (we call this a "trust protector"), and you need to very carefully consider and limit the amendment rights of that person.

Which is better, a stand-alone trust or a testamentary special needs trust?

It really depends on your situation—if one were always best, the other one would never be used! A good special needs estate planning attorney will look at all of the important issues (the child's condition, your overall financial situation and goals, your age, etc.) and will be able to make a recommendation of which type of trust is best for your unique situation.

If my child is currently being well taken care of by public benefits, why would I worry about leaving him any money, especially if it might cause problems?

There are two reasons not to disinherit a disabled child (which is actually a very common, though very poor, approach):

First, there is no guarantee that any public program will continue in acceptable form. Congress and the state legislatures constantly tinker with the rules for qualification for the various programs as well as the services that will be provided. The view of Congress and Courts is that public assistance is not a right, and therefore the level of assistance can be modified or discontinued at any time, for any population. If you have not set up a safety cushion for your child, you are entrusting his or her future to all future federal and state legislators, who may have very different views than you have regarding the acceptable level of services and care for your loved one.

Second, even the services and care provided by the best public assistance programs have huge gaps. One example is dental care, which is not provided. Another is sufficient funding for clothing and shoes, which is not provided. Money in a special needs trust can be used to greatly enhance the quality of life for a disabled beneficiary, but the trust must be set up carefully and adequately funded in order to provide sufficient resources for the beneficiary's changing needs.

If I am planning on leaving a significant Legacy to my disabled child, why would I care if he or she can qualify for public benefits?

Whether you set up a special needs trust is ultimately up to you. However, a parent of a child with special needs should consider two basic facts:

First, the costs of care are impossible to control. Unfortunately, many children with disabilities are more at-risk for further injury, and if a disabled child is further injured, the current costs of care could escalate dramatically. For example, a child with a developmental delay that has interfered with his or her judgment, but who is still relatively independent, might be injured in an automobile / pedestrian accident. If the resulting injuries are severe, that child might need full-time care. If the parents did not take this possibility into account and simply left the child a legacy large enough to meet his or her earlier needs, and if they did not preserve it in a special needs trust, the legacy would need to be spent down until the child was essentially impoverished. Only then would the child qualify for public benefits to meet his or her basic needs. There would be no safety cushion of money to meet his or her other needs. What a waste of the parents' hard-earned legacy!

On the other hand, if the parents' legacy is left for the child's benefit in a special needs trust, it will not need to be spent down, the child could immediately qualify for public benefits to meet his or her basic needs, and the money in the special needs trust could be used to pay those expenses not met by public benefits (clothing, dental care, eyeglasses, recreation, social outings, etc.)

Second, many children with disabilities are vulnerable to people who prey on them. There are many examples of mildly disabled people who inherit money from their parents with no controls (i.e., not in a trust), and who later lose that money to people they considered to be their friends. This will not happen with a correctly formed special needs trust. Because a prudent and experienced trustee is handling the money, the predators cannot simply befriend the beneficiary and gain access to the wealth.

What if a disabled person comes into money; isn't there an alternative to spend-down?

Yes there is—and it is a good thing too, because many disabled people become owners of sufficient property to disqualify them from needed public benefits. Examples of how this might occur are:

- Mother and Father created a UTMA account for the child.
- Grandma left the child money in her will or gave him or her savings bonds.
- The child was somehow injured and received a jury award or settlement.
- The child earned money before he or she became disabled.
- The child wins the lottery.
- Mom or Dad die without a will and the child inherits through intestacy.
- The disabled person is named as beneficiary of an IRA or insurance policy.

There are literally hundreds of ways a disabled person can end up with ownership of enough money to disqualify him or her from receiving public benefits.

In these cases, a parent, grandparent, legal guardian or legal custodian of a person under the age of 65 years can create a "qualified disability trust," which must conform to various rules and regulations. In Colorado (and many other states) this trust must be approved by the local Medicaid agency prior to transferring property into the trust. If the trust is created correctly, and is approved, the disabled person's disqualifying property can be transferred into the trust and the disabled person will then be able to immediately qualify for public benefits.

The disability trust will function as a special needs trust (with a few additional restrictions) to supplement the disabled person's public benefits. However, and this is the large disadvantage of this kind of trust, when the disabled person passes away, Medicaid has a right of repayment for any money expended on behalf of the disabled person during his or her lifetime. In many cases, this will empty out the trust.

Because most disabled people and their families prefer that any money left in the trust upon the death of the disabled person go to other family members, we do not ever want to use a qualified disability trust for planning unless we have to. However, it is a very powerful tool for special needs planning in a situation where a disabled person somehow obtains ownership of disqualifying property.

Besides the trust, what are the other tools in a special needs plan?

The trust will hold and administer the property, but there are other issues that are very important. For example, you will want to nominate the appropriate guardian for the child, even if you think the child will be independent enough to not need a guardian. Even if the child is able to serve as his or her own guardian today, if the child becomes further injured or his or her condition deteriorates, you want to have a guardianship nomination in place.

Another issue is that you may need to have yourself approved as the child's guardian by the court when the child reaches the age of 18. Many parents do not realize they are no longer considered to be the guardians of their children, even significantly disabled children, after the age of 18, unless the court approves a continued guardianship.

You might want to build in an advisory committee for the guardian and trustee, including, perhaps, a medical or other specialist to assist the guardian and trustee in administration of the special needs plan.

You need to decide who the trustees of the trust will be and who can fire the trustee and hire new trustees.

You may want to create a "Letter of Instruction" that will let future guardians and trustees know about the child's background, special needs, special likes and dislikes, capabilities, talents, etc.

In other words, each special needs plan is unique: some people with minor disabilities do not need a guardian; in other cases the parents should nominate three or four successor guardians. In some cases you would use a stand alone trust; in others a testamentary trust works best. That is why it is important to work with attorneys and financial advisors who are very familiar and experienced with special needs planning.

How would a typical plan work?

It will help to explain how a special needs plan works if we take a real-life example: Mom and Dad Jones are in their late 40s and they have three children: Dick, Jane and Bobby. Dick and Jane have no disabilities, are doing well in school, and Mom and Dad expect them to go to college and be self-supporting by the time they reach 23 or 24 years of age. Bobby is their youngest child and was born with a profound developmental delay. Although he is 12 years old, he can only read a few words, has problems with fine motor skills, and cannot perform any math functions at all. Although he is very well adjusted, laughs easily, and in many ways is the center of the family, his parents know that he will never be able to support himself, or even fully care for himself.

Mom and Dad work hard and have a fairly good nest egg set aside for their retirement and their children's education, but they know that they will never be able to also save enough to meet all of Bobby's needs for his entire life.

Mom and Dad might set up a plan that looks like this: They would each create a revocable living trust that takes care of them if they became disabled, and protects the survivor when one of them passes away (see Chapters 3 and

4). The trusts also provide that all of the savings and existing life insurance would be held in trust to care for Bobby and also to educate Dick and Jane and provide for their needs until they reach the age of 25 years or graduate from college. There might be some provisions for additional distributions to Dick and Jane (such as to help them purchase a home, or to pay the expenses of a wedding or childbirth, etc.), but the primary feature of Mom and Dad's legacy is that it will care for Bobby through a special needs trust so that Dick and Jane will not have to financially support him. Uncle Walt and a trust company will be the co-trustees of the trust, with Dick and Jane replacing Uncle Walt when he passes away, or when they reach the age of 30. When Bobby passes away, the money left in the trust will be used to provide a retirement for Dick and Jane, or for their children's education, if Dick and Jane desire.

Knowing that their existing resources might not be enough to care for Bobby for his entire lifetime, Mom and Dad might also create a stand-alone special needs trust, and inform Bobby's grandparents that it is in existence to receive any bequests that would otherwise go to Bobby. In addition, Mom and Dad put $2,000 per year into the trust to pay for a $500,000 life insurance policy that will pay off when the second of them passes away (this has to be done very carefully). Finally, Dad names the trust as the contingent beneficiary on his IRA, so that when he passes away, if Mom thinks she will not need the entire IRA, she can disclaim a portion of the IRA to the trust, where it will grow tax-deferred for Bobby's benefit.

Mom and Dad nominate Uncle Walt as the guardian of all three kids in their will, explicitly stating that Uncle Walt should continue as the guardian of Bobby after the age of 18 as well. Aunt Vivian is named as successor guardian, and younger Uncle Scott is named as third successor guardian (Mom and Dad met with Walt, Vivian and Scott and made sure that they were willing and able to serve as guardians). Dick and Jane (Bobby's brother and sister) are named as successor guardians with priority over Walt, Vivian and Robert once they reach the age of 25 years, provided that they wish to become Bobby's guardians.

Mom and Dad also take all the needed actions to put the other parts of the special needs plan into place, such as including advisory committee provisions in all of their trusts.

This plan is not for everyone. For example, many people want to leave a larger portion of the legacy to Dick and Jane. Some people might want to set aside some portion of their legacy for charity or for grandchildren and great-grandchildren. Each plan is unique, and to be truly successful it must reflect the goals and desires of the person creating the plan—that is how it becomes his or her own true legacy.

In Mom and Dad's case, this plan feels just right. It gives them the sense that they have done all that they can do to balance their desire to create a fulfilling and rewarding life for Dick and Jane with the knowledge that they had to do a little bit more to create a fulfilling and rewarding life for Bobby. They know Bobby's fate will not rest on the whims of Congress and future legislatures, although it will make full use of public benefit programs for so long as those programs furnish acceptable levels of service. They have carefully selected guardians who share their values and love their children (and they discussed it with the guardians ahead of time!)

Estate planning is all about control, and Mom and Dad have done all that they can to control what happens to the most important part of their legacy—their children—and how their wealth will be spent to best enhance that legacy. The reward for good estate planning is simple: it is peace of mind. Mom and Dad sleep better at night with their plan in place.

Chapter 9

- Creditors, Predators and the Need to Protect Yourself -

Everyone wants to protect their legacy for their loved ones to some extent. We discussed several ways to protect your surviving loved ones in Chapter 5. However, some people want to take it a step further and achieve protection of their assets from predators and lawsuits during their lifetime.

Therefore, this Chapter concerns a critically important aspect of estate planning that we call asset protection. It involves placing the ownership, use, and control (or a combination of all three) of an asset into an entity in such a way that the asset itself can be protected against the claims of unknown, unforeseen creditors. That is a mouthful. Here's a simple hypothetical that will help you understand that the need to preserve and protect your assets is an important part of goal setting and legacy building.

Assume you own an apartment building and, fortunately, it experiences nearly full occupancy. You are aware that there are risks associated with your ownership and management of the building. There may come a time when you do not have full occupancy or when other unforeseen circumstances result in your inability to pay the bills. Even more frightening is the prospect of an innocent person being injured on your premises. You are aware that you could be sued. You could even be the object of a lawsuit over an event, for example an automobile accident that you are involved in, that had nothing to do with your apartment building. In almost any case like these, your apartment building will be exposed to the claims that are made against you.

These claimants are currently unknown to you and may even be unforeseeable. Nevertheless, you know that such claims are made every day against people just like you and you know that you may find yourself on the wrong end of a lawsuit with a substantial judgment against you.

Asset protection planning attempts to protect that apartment building (and the other assets that you own) from those future, unforeseen creditors.

Doesn't that have something to do with my moving money out of the United States to another country?

You are referring to what is called "offshore asset protection" which does include moving the ownership of assets to entities that are sited, or located, in foreign countries. Offshore planning is a highly specialized area of estate planning, and is beyond the scope of this book. We will confine our discussion to what is available here within this country, which is called "domestic" asset protection strategies.

Is asset protection planning legal and ethical?

There are certainly some techniques that you probably have heard about that are illegal or unethical, and they usually don't work. However, there are also many techniques that are completely legal and ethical, and that you can employ with a clean conscience. Those are the only kind that ethical planners use. There are simply so many legal and ethical techniques available that it just doesn't make sense not to do asset protection planning correctly.

If I transfer my assets into the name of my revocable living trust, will I get good asset protection?

No, you will not. This is a common misconception, and many people have been disappointed to find out the truth after it is too late. Creating a quality revocable living trust, and transferring your property into the name of that trust, will provide you with enormous benefits (as outlined in earlier Chapters) and it may provide your loved ones with solid asset protection after you die (depending on the provisions you include in your trust, see Chapter 5). However, it will not provide you with any asset protection during your lifetime. This is because you hold the power to revoke or amend the trust, and you are likely to be a current beneficiary of the trust. In Colorado, either one of these facts ensures that a court could subject the trust assets to the claims of your creditors; therefore, a revocable living trust will provide no asset protection for you during your lifetime.

Because of this, if you want to achieve asset protection during your lifetime, you need to follow up your revocable living trust planning with further asset protection planning.

My son is being sued as we speak. Shall we get started right away with some asset protection planning?

There is an important warning, or caveat, that should be understood before beginning any sort of protection planning. Simply put: **YOU CANNOT ENGAGE IN ASSET PROTECTION PLANNING IF THE EFFECT OF THAT PLANNING WOULD BE TO DEPRIVE A KNOWN, EXISTING CREDITOR FROM BEING ABLE TO COLLECT THOSE ASSETS**.

In other words, if your son re-titles his apartment building into an entity, or into someone else's name, with the intent, as the law puts it, "to hinder, delay or defraud" his current and existing creditors, the transaction will be set aside and the asset will be made available to the creditor just as though the transfer had never occurred.

This is because almost every state has some form of "Fraudulent Transfer" act. In Colorado, this law is known as the Colorado Uniform Fraudulent Transfer Act (C.R.S. § 38-8-101, et. seq.). Although this statute is too complex to discuss in full in this book, it is important to understand that it requires asset protection planning to be put in place well in advance of any claims. Violation of this law allows a judgment creditor to recover assets from an asset protection structure.

However, the act also provides a statute of limitations. This means that if your asset protection structure has been in place well in advance of the time the claim arises or becomes known, the creditor will not be able to use the Fraudulent Transfer Act to recover the assets from the asset protection structure.

As you might expect, abiding by this law is often more easily said than done. And that is another reason to exercise care in the selection of your estate planning lawyer. On the one hand, asset protection is a legitimate and honorable component in a free society. For people who are concerned with being good stewards of the properties and assets that have been entrusted to them, protecting their assets from the grasp of currently unknown creditors is a worthy endeavor. On the other hand, hiding what you own so that *existing* creditors cannot locate it or do not know that you own it, is not.

Should I include asset protection strategies as part of my estate planning?

Before answering that question, you need to understand what the word "liability" means: How is it that some outside person has the ability to lay claim to your assets? It is also helpful to understand the varying public policies we see coming out of our judicial system and our state legislatures regarding two competing philosophies: your right to protect your own assets vs. an innocent creditor's right to look to your assets for compensation for injuries he or she received at your hands.

Liability is simply the legal term that means one person is legally responsible for the injuries suffered by another person or that other person's property. For example, suppose that you are driving down the street and a pedestrian unexpectedly steps out in front of you. Suppose you have no time to stop and swerve to miss him, and your quick thinking saves his life. Suppose further that, although you save the pedestrian's life, your swerve causes you to collide with a small sports car driven by a successful plastic surgeon. Finally, suppose that the surgeon is injured just enough so that he can no longer perform the delicate surgery that was his specialty, and he suffers a tremendous loss of income. With the benefit of hindsight, a jury might determine that you could have also avoided the surgeon's car and might enter a judgment against you—indeed, they might enter a sizeable award against you. You then would have "liability" to that surgeon for the entire amount of the jury award. To the extent the judgment exceeds the total insurance coverage you may have, you will be required to pay the balance of the judgment. Unless you can write a check for that amount, the surgeon and his attorney will begin looking for your assets.

Here is a simpler example. Should you fail to make your credit card payment, or if you borrow money, whether it's from your Aunt Matilda or from the First National Bank, you have full liability or responsibility for the unpaid balance including any interest, fees, etc.

In the last few decades, asset protection planning has become more mainstream. While avoiding successful claims by creditors against one's assets has always been important, more people have begun to take a serious look at asset protection planning. Likewise, a number of states have seen the value of such planning and passed laws that permit, even encourage, certain asset protection planning techniques. States have expanded their approach to the tools and strategies of asset protection planning, including trusts and business entities such as corporations and limited liability companies. There are states that, either by legislation, court decisions or both, have made it clear that creditors cannot take assets out of a valid trust or entity to satisfy the creditor's claims against the creator of that trust or owner of that entity. By the same token, there are other states that very much favor helping a creditor get at someone's assets no matter where those assets might be titled.

One result of this philosophical difference is that some states are now competing over which individual state may be the most attractive to new businesses. Legislation providing strong asset protection, favoring a person's ability to protect his or her own assets, is appearing nationwide. Consequently, your discussion with your asset protection attorney may include whether to have your asset protection entities formed in one of these more friendly states. There are, of course, some increased costs involved, but in many situations it can be worth the slightly increased expense.

Asset protection issues must be included in any discussion you have with your estate planning attorney regarding your own particular goals, objectives and legacy building. For some people it may not be a necessary or advisable component, but for nearly everyone it should be an important part of the discussions.

Doesn't insurance take care of most of these issues?

Insurance is one of the important layers of asset protection planning. Most people carry liability insurance on their business, home, automobiles, and other assets. Some people have what is known as umbrella coverage as well. Umbrella coverage is designed to cover liability that either isn't covered in those other forms of insurance or where the limits of the other insurance are too low to pay the claim in full. To the extent there is enough insurance coverage for any given claim, no further asset protection is necessary. However, in many instances one cannot purchase or afford enough insurance to cover all potential liabilities. Further, there can be loopholes or contingencies that allow the insurance company to deny coverage.

Look back to our example of your having a traffic accident involving the successful surgeon. How likely is it that you would have, or could even afford to purchase, enough insurance for that kind of exposure?

It isn't hard to think of such an accident as being somewhat remote. It might in fact be remote. But do we plan for the best of all possible worlds, or do we plan for what we know very well could happen? If our planning is only for the best that could happen, then we really don't need any insurance at all, do we?

When we recognize that catastrophic situations do in fact happen to "somebody", we recognize that we might well be that somebody and that protection planning beyond insurance can be important.

What about exemptions?

Most states provide that certain assets are exempt from the claims of creditors. Again, some states list a great number of assets and provide that the total exemption is relatively high. Other states take an opposite track, providing minimal exemptions. Unfortunately, Colorado has rather limited exemptions.

A listing of assets that are often declared exempt by states could include individual retirement accounts, cash value of life insurance, a person's home, an automobile and oftentimes other personal property. Each state also will limit the value that can be claimed as exempt. For example, one state might provide that a person's residence is exempt, but only up to a total of $50,000. For a person in that state, any equity in the home in excess of the $50,000 would be available to creditors.

What are the best asset protection structures?

A very well known asset protection attorney uses the metaphor of a ladder to describe asset protection planning. The easiest planning technique is what he would call the "bottom rung" of the asset protection ladder. Unfortunately, although inexpensive and easy to implement, it is also the least effective. As you climb the asset protection ladder, each asset protection structure or technique, or rung, provides more effective asset protection than the one below it. However, each step up the ladder involves a bit more complexity and expense than the one below it. You might say, "I want the top rung!" However, you would probably change your tune when you find out that the top rung is expatriation: moving both yourself and all of your assets to a foreign country which has laws that are friendly to asset protection structures. Most clients only want to climb as high as they need to climb in order to achieve solid asset protection. Luckily, you can achieve a relatively high degree of asset protection by climbing only a few rungs up the ladder.

So what are some concrete examples of the need for asset protection?

It is true that anyone can be served with a lawsuit at any time, with or without merit. However, certain professions lead to greater exposure to lawsuits and creditor actions: doctors, lawyers, accountants, business managers, business owners, landlords, financial advisors, engineers and architects. People who are successful in these fields often want to know what they can do to protect their hard-earned assets from predators and creditors.

The owner of a small business is a classic example of one who needs to consider asset protection planning. So is the person who owns investment or commercial real property such as an office building or rental houses or an apartment building. The farmer or rancher who owns some land, livestock, and equipment is another example. Just about anyone owning assets beyond their household furniture and personal toys would be a candidate.

The owner of an investment portfolio has a strong need for protection planning. The options available to successfully protect that kind of asset are somewhat more limited, but strategies do exist and the discussion with a knowledgeable attorney certainly needs to take place.

***Can you provide a hands-on example or specific illustration
of asset protection planning?***

Consider a hypothetical case involving a business owner
and his wife, Bob and Marlene Smith. While it is beyond the
scope of this Chapter to provide technical detail on the
implementation of any protection plan, the situation Bob and
Marlene find themselves in is typical and an overview of one
possible solution is a good example of how domestic asset
protection can work:

> Bob and Marlene have been married for 30 years.
> They are each 55 years of age and have three grown
> children and two grandchildren. Each of their
> children is over 21, married and fully self-supporting.
> Bob and Marlene's estate consists of two apartment
> buildings, three rental houses and a corporation
> that owns and operates a local redi- mix concrete
> company. The corporation, of course, also owns
> trucks, heavy equipment, tools and so forth.
> Additionally, Bob and Marlene own personal assets
> such as their checking account, an investment
> account, their home, and sundry toys. They are
> concerned that their rental properties might be
> exposed to future unforeseen creditors. They are
> not concerned about the redi-mix business because
> they believe they have adequate protection knowing
> that the business assets are owned by a corporation.
> After discussing the concept of liability, Bob and
> Marlene realize that if the corporation, through one
> or more of its employees, commits an act that results
> in liability to an outside person, the corporation and

all of its assets will be available to that creditor. Nothing within the corporation is protected from the corporation's creditors.

Furthermore, if Bob or Marlene is found negligent from an act that has nothing to do with the operation of the business (a short errand to the grocery store), their personal assets are exposed. Not only does "personal assets" include the rental properties, but it includes another asset they own: their stock in the corporation. This sort of an analysis shows Bob and Marlene that they really have very, very limited asset protection. They are currently on one of the lower rungs of the ladder.

Table 1, below, is a straightforward asset protection plan design. It is not the only one; nor, depending on Bob and Marlene's objectives, is it necessarily the best one. However, it is a good example for this hypothetical case.

Limited liability companies (LLCs) may enjoy better asset protection than corporations do, at least in many states. That greater protection results from a legal concept known as the "charging order." That concept constitutes the primary asset protection difference between limited liability companies and corporations. The "charging order" protection, in many states, can prevent a creditor from taking over an owner's interest in a limited liability company whereas the same creditor might be able to take control of the stock in a corporation. That advantage will help you understand the reason for the structure described in Table 1 .

Bob and Marlene's rental properties are titled in three

separate limited liability companies. Their stock in the corporation that runs the business is placed in a fourth LLC. Each LLC is owned by Bob and Marlene (or their revocable trusts).

A fifth LLC is created whose sole function is to do business with the public and to operate the assets owned by the other companies. This "operating company" will not own any of the assets but will lease them from the owner companies, sometimes called holding companies.

In theory, the owner companies will be doing no business with the public whatsoever (they simply lease assets to other companies) and will, therefore, not be engaging in any activity that could create liability to some outside party.

The company that could, and likely will, engage in activity that could create liabilities to others is the operating company. The operating company doesn't own much in the way of assets; at least it does not own the high-value assets that Bob and Marlene want to protect from creditors.

To the extent Bob and Marlene generate *personal* liability, as opposed to business liability, to an outside creditor (the grocery store), the assets within the entities may be protected by the legal concept of the charging order. To go up the ladder and create greater asset protection, Bob and Marlene may choose to put some of their ownership interests in these LLCs into irrevocable trusts. If Bob and Marlene are limited in how they can control and access the assets in the trust(s), a creditor is likewise limited in how he can access the assets.

Table I.

BUSINESS ASSET PROTECTION PLANNING
BOB AND MARLENE SMITH

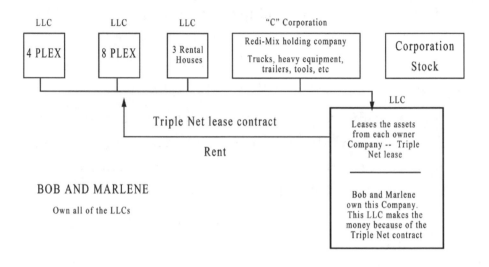

People who engage in this sort of planning must be prepared for a relationship with their planner. Whether it is called a maintenance program or just an ongoing association, and regardless of how it is structured, in order for this kind of asset protection planning to actually produce the intended outcome and result in the protection of assets as described, the structure cannot be neglected or taken for granted. It must be monitored and maintained with an eye for detail. By way of a generalized example: income must be deposited into the right accounts, expenses must be paid from the appropriate accounts, accounting paper trails need to be put in place by the CPA, frequent meetings need to be held, and detailed minutes must be kept. This plan, no matter how beautiful it looks on paper and how highly touted it is by its designer, will simply not work if it isn't nurtured and reviewed.

That may sound like bad news. Most business owners are not in the business of plan maintenance. Bob and Marlene are in the business of running their Redi-Mix operation and managing their investment properties. They do not want to spend their time making sure that all of the T-s are crossed and I-s are dotted in the day-to-day transactions between their various companies.

The good news is far better. The maintenance of this kind of plan is easily accomplished by Bob and Marlene's CPA or by their estate planning attorney. That kind of activity is right up the alley of most professionals. Normally, it is not going to be expensive and the professional paper trail created will be extremely valuable when that unanticipated predator, some years from now, decides to bring a lawsuit.

It is important to understand at the outset that any creditor's lawyer worth his or her salt is going to include every person and entity he or she can imagine in the lawsuit. And the lawyer is going to be experienced and competent in attacking asset protection designs. Careful maintenance on an ongoing basis and a quality paper trail are probably the most important components of any good asset protection plan.

My accountant says that asset protection plans aren't really effective—is she right?

She is partially right—many asset protection plans fail. You may have seen some seminars advertised where a traveling out-of-town promoter indicates that you can attend the seminar and then purchase a small box full of documents that will immediately produce a "bulletproof" asset protection structure. Unfortunately, these structures do not work as advertised, and their failure has caused some very sincere accounting and financial consulting professionals to conclude that asset protection planning simply does not work.

On the other hand, carefully designed asset protection structures, put in place by experienced professionals familiar with state and federal law, and which are carefully maintained by educated clients do, in fact, work—they work in the sense that if the client has a dispute, they will be in a significantly better position to either avoid litigation entirely, to negotiate a much more favorable settlement, or to protect assets from seizure by judgment creditors.

Do asset protection trusts really work?

This Chapter has focused primarily on the use of entities other than trusts. Depending on a person's goals, one or more trusts can be used as effectively as the entities we have been discussing. However, it is important to note that when the rubber hits the road, the asset protection of a trust works because a creditor cannot take what you do not own. So, in order to be comfortable with using trusts as asset protection tools, you have to be prepared for the possibility that now or sometime in the future the assets of that trust will be out of your reach in order to get it out of the reach of your creditors.

There is a proposed law currently making its way through the legislatures of many states that is generically referred to as the *Uniform Trust Code*. Actually, this law is far from uniform, as seen by significant differences in the few states that have adopted it. Almost every state that has adopted it has modified some or many of its provisions. Some experts fear this Uniform Trust Code could destroy the asset protection features of a trust and expose the property placed into the trust not only to your own creditors but to the creditors of your children and other beneficiaries. Others disagree and maintain that the law does not interfere with traditional asset protection planning through trusts.

As with many new laws, the true results won't be known for a while and even then the results of planning in any given state may differ significantly from the results of the same planning in a different state. In the meantime, it is important to put provisions in asset protection trusts that allow them to be "migrated" to a state where better law controls. This is important whether or not the Uniform Trust Code is adopted. At this point in time, Colorado has not adopted any version of the Uniform Trust Code, although various versions have been introduced into the state legislature each year for the past several years.

A newer technique is the use of a "self-settled" asset protection trust (a trust you set up for your own benefit). Until recently, it has not been a viable strategy for domestic planning (although it has long been used in offshore

97

planning). However, in the past few years, several states have enacted laws that specifically permit a person to create a "self-settled" trust: be the beneficiary of the trust (subject to certain standards for distribution), and enjoy asset protection for the wealth that is held within the trust. The statutes in these states specifically set forth the level of asset protection that can be enjoyed, which is fairly high. Unfortunately, Colorado does not have such a law, and "self-settled" trusts created and administered under Colorado law enjoy no asset protection (although a Colorado resident can set up a self-settled asset protection trust in one of the several states that allow such trusts).

The reason you must be very careful with "self-settled" domestic asset protection trusts is that even though another state's law clearly says you can create a "self-settled" trust, be a beneficiary of that trust, and enjoy asset protection, we are only sure that such a trust works for residents of that state whose property is located in that state. For example, if a Colorado resident who creates an Alaska trust is sued in Colorado, and has a judgment entered in Colorado against him, we are not absolutely sure that the Colorado judge will honor Alaska law and the protections set forth in the Alaska trust. A Colorado judge may decide that Colorado does not allow asset protection for "self-settled" trusts and therefore Alaska law does not provide such protection to a Colorado resident either. Either way, the out-of-state domestic "self-settled" asset protection trust could fail as an asset protection device for a resident of Colorado.

Amazingly, even though the laws approving domestic

asset protection trusts have been in effect for several years, and thousands (if not tens of thousands) of these trusts have been established, as of the date of publication of this book, we do not have one single court case where the structure was actually tested and a judge has actually ruled on this question. You could say that this demonstrates how effective these trusts really are, as no judgment creditor has apparently ever pursued the trust far enough to create a reported court case. On the other hand, most planners simply say that it is still an unsettled question.

It is important to remember that you can use irrevocable trusts set up and administered in Colorado for asset protection planning; you simply cannot be a beneficiary of such a trust. If you want to set up a trust where you are not a beneficiary (for example, if you set up a trust for the benefit of your spouse and children) that is not a "self-settled" trust, it has strong asset protection in Colorado, and you can use that trust for very effective asset protection planning. Creating that type of trust also has the benefit of removing the assets transferred into the trust from your taxable estate (if done correctly). This can significantly reduce the impact of estate taxes on your loved ones.

Do offshore trusts really work?

Yes they do. If you put an asset protection structure in place where you create a trust under the laws of a foreign country, and actual title to the trust's assets is held by a trustee (typically a foreign bank or trust company) in a foreign country that has favorable asset protection laws, you can transfer your assets into the trust, be a beneficiary of the trust (subject to certain standards) and enjoy extremely strong asset protection.

However, you have to be very careful in several areas: (1) you need to have a very carefully crafted trust document, drafted by an experienced attorney who understands not only Colorado and United States asset protection law, but also the laws of the selected foreign country; (2) you need to choose the foreign country carefully, some have better laws than others and their laws also change; (3) you want to choose a very solid and reputable trustee with extensive experience in asset protection trusteeship; and (4) you want to ensure that your trustee has absolutely no ties to the United States, does not do business in the United States, and does not engage in any activities in the United States.

Therefore, offshore trust planning, if done correctly, is extremely effective and will provide great peace of mind for someone with significant wealth and who is either in a very high-risk profession or is otherwise truly concerned about liability, creditors and predators. On the other hand, for most people, establishing an offshore trust entails more complexity and cost than they desire, and they find that an entirely domestic asset protection structure, using familiar entities such as limited liability companies, protective trusts and qualified retirement plans gives them the level of protection they need.

What should I do to put an asset protection plan in place?

There is no "one size fits all" asset protection plan—each

plan must be carefully constructed to meet your goals and provide just the level of asset protection you need. As noted before, the "one size fits all" asset protection plan will simply not work (just like with a cheap suit, as we all know, the "one size" actually fits no one). The best way to proceed is to make an appointment with an experienced estate planning attorney who works extensively in the area of asset protection. At that meeting you will be asked to provide information about your goals, values, objectives, situation and asset structure. The planner will then put together an asset protection plan that will meet your unique situation and needs.

Don't be surprised if the planner combines several techniques. For example, your planner may recommend a strongly funded qualified retirement plan, the creation of a limited liability company, and the sale of some of the limited liability company assets to a dynasty trust (see Chapter 16). The planner might also recommend an irrevocable life insurance trust that would protect your life insurance policies (see Chapter 17, Irrevocable Life Insurance Trusts). This would be a common structure that would provide a high degree of protection to a doctor, engineer, architect, business owner or other person in a high-risk profession, and would also provide a high degree of tax reduction as well.

Is an asset protection structure expensive to put in place?

Because each asset protection structure is unique, it is impossible to predict what fee a quality planner would charge in order to design and implement an asset protection structure. Some good news in this regard is that most asset protection structures also provide significant estate tax, and possibly income tax, savings. In many cases, the tax savings alone provide an immediate benefit that is many times the fee the attorney charges to set up the structure. Even if the structure does not produce tax savings, the fees will probably be more reasonable than you would expect and the investment will produce significant peace of mind.

In any event, if you are in a situation where you have a higher than average risk of liability, the cost of failure to plan may greatly exceed the cost of planning.

Chapter 10

- Planning for Your Favorite Charities and Family Foundations -

There are many goals that can be met with charitable giving. Likewise, there are many techniques that fall under the charitable giving umbrella. This Chapter provides the answers to some common questions that arise when thinking about the "hows and whys" of charitable giving:

General Thoughts about Charitable Giving

Q *What are some reasons for making charitable contributions?*
A Gifts to charities achieve philanthropic objectives. They usually provide attractive income and/or estate tax advantages as well. They reflect your values and chronicle much about who you are. It has been said that the best journal of a person's priorities is his or her checkbook. In addition, your own charitable giving can be a way to influence and teach your children about generous living. With proper planning, charitable giving can mark a significant part of the legacy and memory of your life after you are gone.

Q *Are there pitfalls I should think about?*
A It is a sad thing to see good intentions fail. To avoid

common pitfalls resulting from inadequate instructions, poor selection of those who will administer your gift, or simply lack of foresight in thinking things through, great care must be exercised in the planning and creation of charitable gifts. For this reason, even if your charitable giving is modest, it is always important to involve advisors who can impart wisdom as well as knowledge to the planning process.

Other questions may concern the charity itself. Make sure it is tax-exempt and that you have confidence in its integrity and future direction. Obtain as much information as you can. The IRS maintains a current list of tax-exempt organizations at http://apps.irs.gov/app/pub78.

Another suggestion is that you not allow tax considerations to overly influence your charitable giving decisions. Taxes should not be the tail that wags the dog. In other words, tax reasons should serve but not drive the results. Ultimately, charitable giving makes sense only when it serves to advance the causes and ideas that are important to you. If the causes you support are truly important, a tax benefit will be an added incentive. But even if tax reasons are not enough, take time before moving on to weigh whether or not there may be other important reasons for making the charitable gift.

Lifetime Charitable Contributions - Generally

Q   *Where can I obtain some good basic tax information to guide me in making lifetime charitable giving?*
A   A comprehensive and clear resource on charitable contributions is IRS Publication 526.

Q   *What advantage is there in making charitable gifts of appreciated property instead of cash?*

A   If the gift is an appreciated asset, like publicly traded stock or real estate, no capital gains tax is paid by either the charity or the donor when the charity later sells it. The deduction normally equals the value of the gift, but there are exceptions. For example, if the gift is tangible personal property that the charity does not use in connection with its exempt purpose, like artwork, the income tax deduction cannot be more than the cost basis of the asset.

Certain charitable gifts can actually increase your annual income when the income taxes you save in making the gift are coupled with a tax-free conversion of a low yielding to a higher yielding asset. This can happen in a charitable remainder trust, one of the "split interest" gifts discussed below.

Q   *Is there a limit on what I can give to charity?*

A   No, but what you can deduct on your income tax return each year is limited. Your situation may be different, but, generally speaking, in any given year your deduction cannot exceed 50% of adjusted gross income (30% for long-term appreciated assets) with up to five years (state laws vary) to "carry forward" any unused portion of your deduction.

Lifetime Charitable Gifts from Retirement Assets

Q   *I have a tax deferred retirement account and understand that I can use it to make lifetime charitable gifts. Is that true?*

A   Keep in mind that for everyone over 59 ½ years of age who itemizes deductions there has always been a tried and true way to make lifetime charitable gifts from tax-deferred retirement accounts like IRAs and 401k accounts. It works because the deduction can usually offset the taxable income resulting from withdrawing the retirement funds for the gift.

Roth-type retirement funds will not generate taxable income when withdrawn but, assuming you itemize, using them to make charitable contributions still creates a deduction against other income.

Making Charitable Donations through Your Estate

Q   *If I don't think I'll ever have enough to worry about estate taxes, why would I want to consider making gifts to charity upon my death?*

A   If the estate tax exemption remains high, many people who are not concerned about estate taxes will still want to use some of their assets to help a charity that promotes their values. But the shifting landscape of laws in recent years has reminded us with a vengeance that the laws can and do change. Depending on what Congress does, the estate tax could well come back in large and unexpected ways. Those planning their estates who expect to live for decades could die tomorrow. Who can know what the estate tax law will be in the year of your death? Providing charitable gifts in your estate planning assures that if the estate tax does apply, the tax savings of that planning will put your heirs at an advantage. There are ways to structure your charitable gift that it applies only if the gift is needed to avoid or minimize estate taxes.

Q   *Shouldn't I leave my estate to my spouse and let her decide if she wants to make charitable gifts from it?*

A   Gifts to charity are most often designed to occur after the death of both spouses. The concern in deferring the charitable estate gift is to make sure there are sufficient resources to care for the surviving spouse and any dependents. This is not a concern with larger estates. It may also be appropriate to have charitable gifts effective at the death of the first spouse when doing Medicaid planning for small estates.

However, the planning often needs to be done while both spouses are alive and well. One can never predict whether your spouse will be capable of doing additional planning after your death. Also, you may find that you and your spouse are not in full agreement on which charities to support and you may want to ensure that your assets are used to support your choice of charities.

Q   *What about children? When my spouse and I die, shouldn't we leave our estate to our adult children and let them decide how and when they want to make charitable gifts from it?*

A   The tax savings are not as great when your children have the discretion but not the obligation to make a charitable gift at your death. Many times your children will have to choose to make a charitable donation with after tax dollars instead of the before tax dollars that could have been used if you had done charitable planning in your estate plan.

Also, the uncertainties of life can be magnified when grieving the loss of a parent. This is one of the reasons that expecting adult children to make charitable gifts from your estate assets after your death is often unrealistic. If charitable causes are important to you, prudence requires that you consider providing for your charities yourself in the design of your estate plan. Sometimes adult children will make charitable gifts from inheritances. But, even if they do, they may not do so with your priorities and the gifts they make may not be for causes you approve or support.

Thus, it is most appropriate to consider your charitable giving decisions within your overall estate planning before you die.

Q *I have given great thought to my charitable giving desires, and have provided for my favorite charity in my will and trust. Is this all I need to do to make sure a charitable gift will go to my charity after my death?*

A As discussed in Chapter 3, if your assets at death consist of a home in joint tenancy, a retirement account and life insurance, the reality most people do not understand is that the instructions in your will or trust may not have anything at all to do with who ends up with your assets after you die! If you think of the assets as the fuel for your charitable giving, you may have mapped out a great journey but you haven't put any gas in the car to get there.

It is absolutely essential in doing both charitable planning and planning for family and loved ones to consider the question of the titling of your assets. This is something you should not do without the help of a qualified estate planner. It will make all the difference in determining whether or not your intentions and desires are successfully realized after you die. Again, this is a huge issue that goes unheeded for a vast number of people. Your estate plan may do more harm than good in providing for your favorite charity unless you deal with the issues of proper titling.

Sometimes your charitable plan can be structured with something other than an outright gift at your death. This may provide your loved ones with more assets after taxes while keeping the gift to the charity at a value that is the same or higher than the simple gift would have been. This is another reason to consult with your estate planning attorney about how to best achieve your charitable goals.

Q *Can I use beneficiary designations to make charitable gifts after my death?*
A Increasingly, gifts of IRAs and other assets are made at death through beneficiary designation forms. These forms can be obtained from each IRA custodian or investment company. Other assets passing at death by beneficiary designation may include bank accounts, mutual fund and other brokerage accounts, and life insurance. The caution here is the very same as in the answers to some of the last questions. Charitable and other gifts need to be thoroughly coordinated, and this will only happen through comprehensive

planning done with the advice of a qualified estate planning attorney.

Q   *Does it make any difference what kind of assets are used from my estate to make charitable gifts after my death?*
A   Choosing to make estate charitable gifts with IRAs and other tax-deferred assets will allow your heirs to entirely avoid paying both the estate tax and the ordinary income tax that will otherwise be generated after your death. Other assets with this advantage include accounts receivable from a sole proprietorship business, unpaid salary, and accrued interest on bonds.

Q   *How do I gift an IRA or other assets to charity at death to avoid the income tax?*
A   Check with your estate planning attorney whether your IRA or other assets have beneficiary designation forms that determine their distribution at your death. The process needs to start by making sure that it is coordinated and fits with your overall estate plan. If you want to name your charity as beneficiary on the designation form, it is important to make sure that you are doing so correctly and that the designation is accepted by the administrator or other proper person handling the designation.

Q   *How are assets handled if I have a living trust? If I want to leave them to charity, should I name my trust or should I name my charity on my designation forms?*
A   Charitable giving is best handled within or in close coordination with your revocable living trust. It cannot be

over-emphasized that whether or not you have a living trust, you must thoroughly coordinate all the various tools that may be involved in your charitable gifts, including your will, trust, "pay on death" designations and beneficiary designations, because they will all have an impact on the disposition of your assets upon death. For example, your attorney will want to design your estate plan to make sure it receives the full charitable deduction. The full amount of the gift you want to make should pass to the charity unreduced by taxes, expenses and other estate charges that can inadvertently be allocated to the gift.

Using Family Foundations and Donor Advised Funds to Make Charitable Gifts

Q *What is a family foundation?*

A A family foundation, also called a private foundation, is a non-profit charitable entity that receives its donations from a family or group of other private individuals rather than from appealing to the public at large. Typically, the foundation is created or established by the donor group. It is typically non-operating, which means that it does not conduct charitable programs or activities. Instead, it supports other charities that do so by giving at least a required minimum amount of its assets each year to operating charities such as hospitals, religious groups and others. The private donor group oversees and administers the affairs of the family foundation, including investments and the decisions regarding distribution of its assets to one or more operating charities of its choosing.

Q   *Why do people form and use family foundations? Couldn't families give directly to their favorite charities instead of giving through an intermediate family foundation?*

A   Yes, and with the same or better tax benefits. But they decide to form and work through a family foundation for various reasons. For example, using the family name as part of the name of the foundation can enlist a desired sense of intergenerational togetherness within the family. Also, family members are naturally drawn to opportunities to work together to contribute to the common cause by serving on the board of the foundation, for example.

The foundation can also be effective in teaching philanthropic values to younger members of the family. Within limits, foundation funds can be used to pay salaries and expenses of family members. The synergy of a family or other group working together can achieve great things in advancing charitable priorities.

Q   *Are there downsides to forming a family foundation?*

A   Yes. There are legal and accounting costs in set up, administration and annual tax return filings. Tax limitations include a tax deduction limited to 20% of adjusted gross income for donation of appreciated assets and 30% for other assets (compared to 30% and 50% limits that apply to other charitable entities). Moreover, the deduction of appreciated assets (except publicly traded stock) is calculated at cost basis rather than current value.

In addition, a private foundation is subject to a 2% excise tax on net investment income. Annual distribution to charitable causes must equal at least 5% of a private foundation's asset value.

Q *I've heard that "donor advised funds" are an alternative to charitable giving through a family foundation. Is that true, and how do they work?*

A Yes. A donor advised fund is created through a non-operating public charity whose primary purpose is to manage, administer and disburse charitable funds. Some well-known companies, such as Fidelity and Vanguard, have related charitable organizations for this purpose.

The donor makes an irrevocable gift to the charitable organization, resulting in an immediate charitable tax deduction. The gift proceeds remain in a special fund identified with the donor. They are invested and can be accumulated tax free, like an endowment. The charitable organization allows the donor to request at any time that some or all proceeds in the donor fund be paid out to an operating charity. The organization sometimes makes the investment decisions but allows the donor to advise when and how much is paid out and for what charitable purposes. The donor may advise disbursement among any number of charities in any desired proportions or amounts.

A donor advised fund can serve as a temporary parking place for gift proceeds while the donor decides when, how much, and to which charities distributions will be made. For example, a donor may wish to avoid or offset recognition of income (perhaps a bonus or capital gain) at the end of a tax year. If income is expected from the sale of an appreciated asset, the donor will donate all or part of the asset to the donor advised fund before the sale in order to avoid capital gains tax. Giving into a donor advised fund before year end creates a charitable deduction against that year's income, while reserving time until the following year or years to make distribution decisions.

Donor advised funds are a good alternative to private foundations in certain situations. They possess many of their advantages, such as tax-free growth of the donated proceeds and ability to make annual charitable distributions, but without some perceived disadvantages.

Advantages of private foundations not available through donor advised funds include more donor control, a more prominent connection between family name and philanthropy, a wider range for which the donated proceeds may be used, and the ability to pay reasonable compensation and expenses relating to foundation activities from the donated proceeds.

Split Interest Charitable Gifts

Q   *What are lifetime split-interest gifts and how do they work?*

A   A "split-interest" charitable gift divides gift benefits between a donor (or persons designated by the donor) and one or more charities. They often involve gifts of highly appreciated assets. Split-interest giving achieves both personal and charitable objectives. A donor may give stock, avoiding capital gains tax and getting a tax deduction for the gift portion, while reserving lifetime income on the value of the stock. Or a donor who only occasionally uses an asset, like a vacation home, might give the property to charity, reserving the right to use it at certain times each year.

Donors normally make split-interest gifts during lifetime, but can also sometimes do so at death. Except for deposit agreements, split-interest gifts cannot be cancelled once made.

Q　*What are some different kinds of split-interest gifts?*

A　Split-interest gifts come in various kinds. Some not discussed below, because of their more limited application and popularity, are life estates, pooled income funds, and charitable lead trusts. We'll look at three others, which are gift annuities, charitable remainder trusts, and deposit agreements.

Q　*I'm told that gift annuities are a good idea for older people. Why would I consider a charitable gift annuity and how would I go about doing so?*

A　Charitable gift annuities have two essential features. First, they are an investment contract between a donor and the issuing charity. In return for the gift, the charity pays to one or two "annuitants" (designated by the donor) fixed income, usually on a quarterly basis, usually for the remaining lifetime of the annuitant. A gift annuity is also a charitable gift. The donor makes an immediate gift to charity, and the portion that the IRS predicts will go to the charity results in a tax deduction.

Charities usually have their own gift annuity programs.

They offer gift annuities in minimum gift amounts, which are typically $10,000. Under charitable remainder trusts, the donor rather than the charity creates the trust and typically pays the cost of doing so.

From a donor perspective, gift annuities are simple. They do not offer the flexibility of charitable remainder trusts. However, especially for smaller gifts, simplicity makes them a popular choice.

The annuity income depends on gift value, the ages of the annuitants at the time the annuity is issued, the date distributions begin and end, and, usually, rates recommended by the American Council on Gift Annuities.

Older donors qualify for higher rates of return. However, as discussed below, high rates are also available to younger donors who decide to delay the receipt of income.

If an appreciated asset is donated for income tax purposes, the income distributions are a blend of return of principal, capital gain, and ordinary income (depending on the asset).

Cash or publicly traded stock is often used to fund a gift annuity. Gifts of tangible personal property, like artwork and airplanes, although unlikely, can be used to fund a gift annuity and qualify for an immediate tax deduction. Other assets could include life insurance policies with cash values that are no longer needed by the family. Closely held stock, either "C" or "S," as well as encumbered real estate, may also be considered in some cases.

A so-called "flexible deferred gift annuity" offers a powerful, simple alternative to remainder trusts and to ordinary gift annuities, especially for younger donors. Here, the donor (usually younger than retirement age) makes a gift in return for an annuity that will not pay income until a future date, such as the annuitant's projected retirement date. The result is more income because the charity will have been able to invest and grow the asset tax-free during the deferral period. A key feature is that the donor can decide at any time when to begin to receive income.

It is also possible with some limitations to "commute" payments so they start and are fully paid during a specified window period, such as during a child's or grandchild's years in college, when income needs are greater.

Q *What is a deposit agreement?*

A Of the "split interest" vehicles we are discussing, only the deposit agreement may be freely cancelled or changed at any time. A deposit agreement is a special arrangement between a donor and a charity. The charity provides the form of agreement, which is usually negotiable. One essential feature is that the donor can at any time withdraw some or all of the gift assets and even most terms of the agreement during the donor's lifetime.

Q *Why would the donor decide to withdraw funds after "giving them" to charity?*

A There are many reasons including future personal needs, unexpected medical care for children or aging parents, or simply a change of mind in charitable gift planning. The "gift" is incomplete, meaning that the donor can always cancel it. Of course, there is no charitable tax deduction unless and until the gift becomes permanent.

Q   *How do deposit agreements work?*

A   The donor in cooperation with a charitable beneficiary creates a trust agreement, under which the charity agrees to act as trustee. The donor may name the charity as well as other favorite charities to receive trust income and principal. Little or no donor expense or time is involved in either set-up or administration. Unlike a charitable remainder trust, no special tax returns or other filings need to be prepared. The gift proceeds remain in trust until the donor decides to withdraw them or to release them to charitable use.

During the trust term, charitable distributions are made in amounts and at times determined by the donor and the charity under the agreement. The donor receives a tax deduction when distributions are made. At a future designated time, usually the donor's death, the trust distributes the remaining trust assets to the charity, the trust ends, and donor's estate receives an income and estate tax deduction for the donation.

The arrangement is simple. It is particularly attractive to donors who are not concerned with receiving an income tax deduction when the trust is set up and funded. Although retaining maximum ability to revoke or amend, the donor receives recognition from the charity when the trust is set up and funded—and enjoys ongoing satisfaction by supporting the charity's work annually or as often as the distributions are made.

Q   *What is a charitable remainder trust and how does it work?*

A   Unlike a gift annuity, a charitable remainder trust is typically established by a donor rather than by a charity, and is administered by a trustee of the donor's choosing. It is a private transaction, the expenses of which are paid by the donor or from the trust, many times without the involvement or even the knowledge of the charities named as beneficiaries.

Highly appreciated, low-income-producing donated assets produce the greatest tax benefits. The trustee usually sells the assets after they have been donated and invests the proceeds for higher returns. With some limitations, the donor may act as trustee and direct the sale as well as future investments.

A trust may have an unlimited number of income beneficiaries (normally the donor or family members) who receive income payments for life, or for fixed terms not exceeding 20 years. The annual income must be at least 5% of the initial gift value but no more than 50%. Besides the 50% limitation, the present value of the charitable gift remainder interest, as defined by IRS guidelines, must be at least 10% of the value of the assets that fund the trust. At the end of the term, all remaining trust proceeds are distributed to charity.

Professional trustees, including community foundations, can be hired to administer the trust or serve as trustee for a fee. The trustee must file income tax returns and reports. Some advise that in order to justify the effort and expense of set-up and administration, the gift value should be at least

$100,000. Depending on donor objectives, the flexibility afforded by remainder trusts may justify smaller gift values. However, smaller gifts are often better suited to gift annuities. Another reason to consider a gift annuity is risk. In the event of insolvency, neither the income beneficiaries nor the charity can look beyond the charitable remainder trust assets for payment, except for trustee malfeasance. A gift annuity is backed by all of the assets of the issuing charity.

Q   *What flexibility is afforded using a remainder trust?*

A   The trust can pay a fixed (annuity) amount each year (determined as a percentage of the original gift value) or a varying unitrust amount (under which the payment from the trust is a set percentage of the trust assets, as determined at the end of each year, for example, 6%).

If the trust earnings in a given year are lower than the unitrust interest (for example if the earnings were less than 6% in a given year), a unitrust can pay the actual "net income" for that year rather than the higher designated unitrust percentage (which would require the sale of trust assets). It can also include what is known as a "make-up" provision. That is, along with the trust being required to pay the percentage return each year only if there is income sufficient to do so, the donor can require that any deficit be made up in later years if additional extra income is earned.

A unitrust can start out as a "net income" trust that then "flips" to a straight unitrust. This has advantage when dealing with a hard-to-sell asset generating little or no income. The trust in this case would start out as a "net income" unitrust to give the trustee time to sell it. After a defined triggering event (such as the sale of the "unmarketable" asset), the unitrust would "flip" to a straight percentage unitrust, from that point on guaranteeing the beneficiaries a desired fixed percentage of annual trust value.

Q *Can the donor of a charitable remainder trust reserve the right to change the identity of the charitable beneficiaries at any time?*

A Yes. That can be a big advantage over using charitable gift annuities.

Q *Are there limits on using mortgaged or encumbered property as gift assets in a charitable remainder trust and other split-interest gifts?*

A Debt-encumbered assets may not be appropriate unless they are of a non-recourse nature. The reason is that the trust will be deemed to bestow a prohibited benefit to the donor (as the trust pays off the debt, it relieves the donor of liability). Solutions are to pay the debt off with current funds or borrowed funds secured by other assets, a lien release in return for other security, or possibly an "UPREIT" in which the asset is first transferred to a partnership in return for unencumbered limited partnership shares.

Q *What other kinds of property are inappropriate for charitable remainder trusts?*

A "S" corporation stock cannot be used to fund a charitable remainder trust, but can work for a gift annuity. However, remainder trusts work well with hard-to-value assets (like closely held "C" stock) that would not work with gift annuities. If tax-exempt bonds are the gift investment, or if the donor insists that the investment otherwise be limited to a particular form, a remainder trust and not a gift annuity must be the vehicle of choice.

Q *What other ways distinguish charitable remainder trusts from gift annuities?*

A Remainder trusts can be set up beforehand, and funded at death. This is generally not recommended with gift annuities. The assets upon death could include highly appreciated non-qualified stock options and other assets, which carry unique income tax treatment.

Chapter 11

- Planning for Animal Companions -

It is not unusual for a client to want to make provisions for beloved animal companions. Many estate plans have some provisions for who will take care of the family pets. However, for some people this issue is of paramount importance—some people clearly treasure their relationship with their animal companions to a very high degree. They want to make absolutely sure that their dogs and cats are well cared for. In other cases, the client's animal companion has a life expectancy that greatly exceeds theirs, and it simply makes sense to provide for the beloved horse, parrot or even potbellied pig.

For example, a woman named Joan who lives in a small town north of Denver owns a beautiful Macaw (a large member of the parrot family) named Jose. Joan is in her 60s, and Jose is in his teens—and a remarkable teenager he is: he talks, he greets visitors, and he provides great entertainment. Jose has already survived his first companion, an elderly gentleman who derived much enjoyment from Jose's companionship and gave Jose to Joan shortly before his death. Joan also greatly enjoys Jose, loves his companionship, and realizes the responsibility she faces, as Jose has a life expectancy of up to 80 years! It is entirely possible that Jose will live with Joan for a much longer time than her own children lived with her and, in fact, Jose could outlive Joan's children (it is amazing what a good diet and lack of stress will do for you). Obviously, Joan feels that Jose requires long term planning, and she is very concerned. She feels much like a mother with a dependent child might feel.

Many clients feel the same way about a beloved horse, dog or cat.

Although it is a new field, because it is so important to their clients, most quality estate planners consider planning for animal companions to be serious business, and work with their clients to include high quality animal companion planning in their clients' estate planning. Because it gives clients such great peace of mind, this work can be very rewarding.

Is it legal to make provisions for animals in your estate plan?

Luckily for Jose, times have changed and there are now laws which make it clear that planning for animals can be done effectively. For many years there was a legal principle that only human beings could be the beneficiaries of trusts. Over the years, the various legislatures have addressed this issue and in 1995 the Colorado legislature passed C.R.S. § 15-11-901, which specifically allows the creation of trusts that benefit animals, commonly called "Pet Trusts."

In addition, because animals are considered personal property, you can pass ownership of animals in your will or revocable living trust, and make provisions for contingent ownership in the event that your first choice declines to take an animal or predeceases you.

Finally, although there is no statutory provision that expressly sets forth that you can make provisions for the care of your animal companions in the event of your disability, the statutes that govern powers of attorney (C.R.S. § 15-14-501, et. seq.) state that you can make provisions regarding the care and maintenance of your personal property, so it is now possible to include provisions in a person's durable power of attorney that name an animal caregiver who has the power to care for the animals, expend the owner's money on food and veterinary care, etc.

How can I ensure that my animal companions are cared for if I become disabled?

The first thing you need to do is ensure that your disability planning does not consist of form documents; you will need to have your attorney alter the typical durable power of attorney to include provisions for the care of your animal companions.

The most important thing to do is to select a caregiver, or "agent," who will care for the animals in the way you desire. You need to select the caregiver carefully, as they could end up with the animals for a fairly long time if you have an extended illness or incapacity. It is a good idea to choose at least two, and preferably three, caregivers, and rank them in the order of preference (in order to avoid argument).

Next, you need to mandate (not "wish" or "desire" or any other wishy-washy words) that the financial agent under the power of attorney provide sufficient funds for the care of your animals. You can list specific needs, but also leave it somewhat open ended as in "and any other expense which my veterinarian shall deem reasonable." Obviously, your values will dictate these provisions, just as your values dictate the provisions in the rest of your planning. For example, some people really feel that their animals require the best of all possible medical treatment, while other clients want to put limits on medical expenditures. It is up to you, and your attorney can help you articulate the correct wording.

The document should make it clear that the caregiver has the authority to remove the animal companion from your home and to either take it into the caregiver's home or to make other suitable arrangements for care.

You also need to put language in the power of attorney that specifically says that your animal caregiver has the right to go to court to enforce the provisions of the power of attorney, and that they can recover attorney fees and costs from anyone who contests the provisions in your power of attorney regarding the care of your animals.

Next, you should prepare a separate letter, which is not really a legal document, that outlines the various needs of your animal companions and your wishes regarding individual care, such as socialization, exercise, diet, etc.

Finally, you need to give a duly executed duplicate original of the power of attorney to each of the people you have selected as caregivers.

Why do you suggest such formality?

In a perfect world all of your family members and other loved ones would understand your love for your animal companions, and would honor your request to provide them with good food and veterinary care. In some cases, there is such a perfect world. However, in many other cases, the loved ones who stand to eventually inherit your wealth might view your provisions for quality care of your animal companions as a waste of their inheritance, and might seek to deny the caregiver the level of funds you have specified. You do not want your provisions for your animal companions to cause disputes and strife among your loved ones, so the best route is to put your precise intentions into legally binding documents, make sure that such documents are legally enforceable, and ensure that the right people have valid duplicate originals of those documents. These three criteria should be sufficient to head off disputes from disgruntled heirs.

Again, you absolutely must be clear about your unique situation and the unique solution you want to put in place. This is no time for a one-size-fits-all form document! Your unique voice must come through clear and strong in the documents if you want your intentions to be honored.

What can I do about my animals if I die?

First, you need to talk to the people who you would like to take your animal companions—find out if they are willing, and if they will have any requirements that your plan must cover. This may not be much of a concern for a poodle, but if you want someone to take your seven thoroughbred horses, you need to find out if your chosen people can accept them, or if they can only accept them if you provide funds for boarding and care. Again, it is a good idea to list at least three people who have indicated a willingness to take the animals — you never know what circumstances might prevent your first choice from taking the animals.

Second, you need to carefully formulate a plan for the care of the animals. Again, if you are planning for a poodle, a cat or a parakeet, the person you have selected may be willing to simply take the animal and provide for its future care and feeding from his or her own funds. The same may be true of even larger animals. However, it may be that the very best person to take your horse (in terms of availability, love, concern and agreement with you on the issues of care) does not have the financial capability to care for the horse properly. In such a case, you need to make financial arrangements.

Therefore, the first step is to leave the animals to the right people and the second step is to put a solid, definite, plan into place. You would put these provisions in either your will or your revocable living trust (or perhaps in both). Again, it is impossible to emphasize too greatly how important it is to be clear and firm in these bequests, and to make them properly — you do not want any disputes on these issues.

How do I ensure that there are adequate funds to take care of my animal companion?

You can simply make outright cash bequests in your will

or revocable living trust coupled with the gift of the animal. For example, you could say "I give my horse, Trigger, to my niece, Chelsea McDaniel, along with the sum of $10,000 for Chelsea to use for the care and maintenance of Trigger. If for any reason Chelsea shall be unwilling or unable to accept Trigger, then both of these gifts shall lapse and I give Trigger to my nephew, George McDaniel, along with the sum of $10,000 to be used for the same purposes."

The only potential problem with this approach is such language in a will or revocable living trust is not binding. It could be that Chelsea, despite her big heart, is not a great money manager, and despite her best intentions the $10,000 gets spent on a pickup truck and she later discovers that she cannot financially afford to take good care of Trigger, and she has to sell him to a stranger.

Suppose, on the other hand, that Chelsea behaves wonderfully, but unexpectedly passes away. The $10,000 goes to her heirs at law, along with Trigger, and your wishes are entirely disregarded.

The potential problem with the outright gift is that it gives up a significant level of control. Instead you would probably want to create a Pet Trust: You would name a suitable person as trustee of a trust for Trigger, and have that person hold the money and release it to Chelsea specifically for expenditures for Trigger's benefit. It is very important that the trustee be entirely neutral. For example, it should not be Chelsea's mother (unless her mother has really earned your respect and has impeccable character). In addition, the trustee usually should not be the remainder beneficiary under the trust (in other words, when Trigger dies, you usually do not have the money that is left in the trust go to the trustee). Unless you are absolutely sure of the trustee's character, that situation could create too much of a conflict of interest, and there would be too much temptation for the trustee to be stingy with Trigger's care. What you want is a trustee who has no financial incentive to be either too generous or too conservative. Various family members, your accountant, a fellow horse owner, all might make excellent trustees—your attorney can assist you.

Who should get the money left in the trust when Trigger dies? It could be Chelsea, but only if you know in your heart of hearts that this would not cause her to be stingy with Trigger's care. It could be other people who have no stake in Trigger's care, or it could be a gift to a charity that furthers humane treatment of animals, or funds equine therapy for disabled children or conservation easements for riders. It's your Legacy; make it worthwhile!

This planning makes good sense for a horse, but the same principle applies whether you are setting up a trust for a horse, dog, cat, pig or parrot. The primary difference is that the cost of care varies widely depending on the type of animal. For example, a young horse might require a much larger trust than an older dog. In this respect, your veterinarian can assist you in determining what a lifetime of care will likely cost.

Can I compensate the caregiver?

Sure you can—you simply have to make provisions in

your durable power of attorney (for compensation while you are disabled) and in your will or revocable living trust (for compensation after you pass away). Be sure to be specific: you can leave a lump amount, a monthly amount, or make whatever arrangements you wish.

However, simply because you can legally compensate your caregiver does not mean it is a good idea. You should carefully ask yourself the question: "Do I want a caregiver who is serving because they get paid, or who is serving because they love my animal?" You may want to make provisions for modest compensation to encourage good quality care, but you should think carefully before you make provisions for significant compensation. You want Chelsea to ride Trigger because she loves to ride him, not because she has to ride him in order to get her paycheck: she will telegraph her attitude to Trigger either way, and that attitude will certainly affect his quality of life. On the other hand, if Chelsea is a busy single mother who simply cannot afford to take time off from her job to ride Trigger unless the trust provides supplementary income, she might express that joy every time she gets in the saddle. Every case is different and you are the only person who knows Chelsea, Trigger and your attitude towards both.

Are there any other issues we need to think about?

Your unique situation will determine the issues your plan needs to address. However, there are a few issues that commonly arise:

First, be sure to carefully identify your pets in your

documents by marking brand, breed, etc. Don't assume that everyone knows that the grey cat is Casey and the black cat is William; describe them carefully. On the other hand, if you are giving all of your pets to someone, you can simply say "all of my pets" or "all of my animal companions."

Second, think about whether you want to specify what will happen to the remains when your pet dies. Do you want to specify burial or cremation, or do you want to just leave it up to the caregiver?

Third, if you create a Pet Trust, give some thought to how you feel about heroic measures and end of life issues. Do you want every last cent to be spent on care, or do you want to specify that euthanasia is acceptable when your animal's quality of life has declined? Bear in mind that making this decision is much easier on the decision maker if he or she is not the one who receives whatever money left in the trust.

Fourth, and this bears repeating, make sure that you name backup caregivers and trustees, especially if the animal has a long life expectancy.

Can I set up a foundation to care for animals?

Absolutely, and sometimes it makes very good economic sense. If you want to leave funds to specific public charities, you can do so. However, if you want to set up a foundation that can pick and choose which charities it will support, and can shift it's giving from one charity to another in response to shifting needs, you can create your own foundation. If you set it up at your death, it is called a testamentary foundation and will allow your estate to deduct any monies you leave to the foundation from your taxable estate. This can lead to a significant saving on estate taxes. Even better, if you set your foundation up during your lifetime, you can deduct contributions made to the foundation during your life on your current income tax return (within certain limits). This approach will not only save on estate taxes but will reduce current income taxes!

In addition, because a qualified private foundation is treated as a charity, you could make a private foundation be the remainder beneficiary of your charitable remainder trust, the income beneficiary of a charitable lead trust, etc. There are many possibilities and many techniques not only to establish a truly meaningful Legacy, but to also achieve significant tax savings and to substantially leverage tax opportunities. Those approaches are detailed in Chapters 10 and 13.

Chapter 12

- Planning for Earlier Medicaid Qualification -

Many people are concerned about the rising cost of nursing home care. In 2011, the average cost of nursing home care in the Denver area was nearly $7,000 per month, and the costs are increasing at a rate of three to five percent per year. If costs continue to increase at the rate of five percent per year, in 2016, the average monthly cost will be $8,954 per month, which is more than $107,000 per year.

Obviously, the best way to pay these potentially devastating costs is to pass them on to an insurance company, by obtaining long term care insurance before care is needed. However, even though this is the preferable route, many people either cannot get long term care insurance due to a pre-existing condition, or wait too long to apply, and eventually become uninsurable. Just as it is impossible to purchase fire insurance after your home catches fire, you cannot wait until you need long term care insurance to purchase it.

The next best way to cover long term care costs is to have the Medicaid program pay some, or all, of those costs. Medicaid will pay these costs; however, because it is a public benefit program, it requires that you expend nearly all of your own resources before it will step in and pay the remaining costs.

Because of this, and with the huge potential costs of long term care looming, many people worry that even a substantial savings account will be wiped out if they, or their spouse, need such care. Therefore, many people who cannot get long term care insurance want to know whether they can plan ahead so that they will qualify for Medicaid-financed long term care before they are financially completely wiped out. The answer is a very qualified yes, but only with good planning, which must be put in place well before long term care is needed.

Why is advance planning necessary?

The reason advance planning is now very important is that in February of 2006, Congress and the President enacted into law some very sweeping reforms of the Medicaid eligibility rules, which made it much more difficult to qualify for Medicaid long term care benefits, and which eliminated quite a few Medicaid planning strategies that planners had been employing to assist clients. Those changes also severely penalize people who engage in the newly-prohibited planning techniques after February 8, 2006—techniques that had been used legally for years, and that have been published in many books and magazines. However, even under the new 2006 rules, planning that is accomplished well in advance will still work.

The silver lining to this cloud is that the same February 2006 law that made Medicaid qualification so difficult included one very good provision, which is that the states are allowed to set up cooperative Long Term Care Insurance arrangements between Medicaid and private insurance companies. Colorado has enacted such an arrangement, and the arrangement is very beneficial for people who want to plan. In essence, the program allows people to retain a higher level of assets and still qualify for Medicaid long-term-care benefits, if they also purchase a qualified Long Term Care Insurance Policy. For example, if George and Mary Planner each purchase a qualified Long Term Care Insurance Policy that will pay up to $200,000 in benefits, and George needs long term care that exceeds the $200,000 in benefits from the insurance company, then Mary will be able to retain an additional $200,000 in personal assets and still qualify for Medicaid benefits for George than would ordinarily be the case. A qualified policy does not usually cost any more than a non-qualified policy, so there is no reason not to ensure that any policy be qualified. Obviously, if you can qualify for Long Term Care Insurance, this is a very attractive opportunity.

This program is subject to change and is always evolving, so it is important to consult with a qualified attorney and a knowledgeable Long Term Care Insurance Agent prior to making a decision that depends upon this provision in the law.

A word of caution: what Congress did in February 2006, it can do again at any time—this is an area where the law not only is subject to change—it is an area where the law is sure to change. Therefore, it is absolutely imperative that if you choose to do Medicaid planning, you engage an attorney who is experienced in this area, and who regularly prepares

Medicaid qualification plans. Do not be shy about asking how many Medicaid qualification plans an attorney prepares each year. If he or she does not prepare at least one or two such plans each month, and if he or she does not confirm to you that he or she is intimately familiar with the most current rules and regulations, be sure to find a different attorney. This is an area where you definitely need experienced and up-to-date counsel.

For this same reason—the fact that the laws and rules change constantly—you should never rely upon published material in order to implement a Medicaid qualification plan, including the material found in this Chapter of this book! This Chapter, as well as other written materials, may be useful for background information. But before you engage in any actual planning, be sure to meet with an experienced attorney and engage that attorney to design and implement that plan. This is definitely not an area where you want to try and do it yourself—the risks are simply too great.

Is Medicaid planning legal and ethical?

Medicaid planning is simply the structuring of your assets in such a way that you or your spouse can legally qualify for Medicaid benefits sooner than you would qualify if you did not engage in planning. The kind of planning discussed in this Chapter does not entail "hiding" assets or engaging in any other kind of unethical behavior. Most people who do Medicaid planning are law-abiding and ethical people, and attorneys have sworn to uphold a code of ethics in their representation of those clients. Therefore, a qualified attorney will not have any intention of doing anything that is not fully legal and proper.

There is a fundamental misunderstanding of Medicaid planning. The public image (fostered by the media) of the typical Medicaid planning client is the image of a millionaire who secretly transfers all of his or her assets to a cohort, so that he can freeload off of the taxpayers and receive luxurious long term care free of cost. The reality is nothing of the sort.

The actual Medicaid planning client is typically a hard-working middle-class couple who has managed to accumulate a savings account and is counting on that money to provide for a "safety net" in retirement for themselves. For some reason, they cannot obtain or cannot afford long term care insurance, and realize that if one of them were to require an extended stay in a nursing home, the cost of nursing home care would entirely wipe them out within a few short years. They know that Medicaid will require them to be entirely impoverished before it begins paying long term care benefits, and they are frightened about what will happen to the spouse who does not have to go into the nursing home. They want to plan so that they can provide some sort of continuing "safety net" for that spouse.

Attorneys who practice in this area believe that it is perfectly ethical to help those clients preserve a safety net, so that the spouse who is not disabled will not risk becoming completely destitute in the event his or her spouse needs extended long term care. Good planners will carefully follow the law, and will fully disclose all of the planning to Medicaid, so that they and their clients can sleep soundly at night.

Isn't Medicaid nursing home care inferior to private-pay care?

Generally, the level of care is exactly the same. It is important to understand that Medicaid is paying the bills for roughly half of the people in long term care facilities. The reimbursement from Medicaid, while not extravagant, is adequate to allow the facilities to stay in business and make a profit, so most facilities want to attract and keep clients who are receiving Medicaid benefits. The problem is that Medicaid will cap the number of Medicaid qualified residents that any long term care facility can accept. If the facility has reached that number, it cannot accept another Medicaid applicant without permission from Medicaid.

The effect of this is that many desirable long term care facilities, especially those with convenient metro-area locations, are simply unable to accept any more Medicaid residents. What this means is that the less-desirable long term care facilities, or the ones with inconvenient locations, are the ones with space to accept Medicaid qualified clients. When children tour facilities that have space available, this can sometimes lead to the impression that Medicaid-financed care is lower in quality.

The solution to this problem is the application of shoe leather. There are usually always some spaces left in high-quality long term care facilities that are approved for Medicaid, but they may not be easy to find. You may have to forego the convenient metro area location and look further into the outer suburbs, or even into the smaller towns a bit further away in order to find a high quality long term care facility that can accept another client receiving Medicaid benefits.

One technique attorneys often employ is to intentionally select a high-quality long term care facility with good facilities and staff, and then budget for a period of private pay (where the applicant pays the bills from his or her own money). In most Medicaid qualification plans created since February of 2006, there will be some period of private pay in any event. When the client later becomes eligible for Medicaid benefits, the long term care facility will either already have the ability to take another client under Medicaid payment, or will seek a temporary waiver of the limit until an additional Medicaid space becomes available. It is much easier for a facility to turn away a client who is qualified for Medicaid than it is to reject a client that they have come to know and appreciate. In addition, the impending Medicaid qualification is no surprise to the long term care facility administrator— the planner has very often alerted the facility staff to the exact day that the client will qualify for Medicaid, and the staff has had time to make arrangements with Medicaid.

Therefore, it is quite possible to obtain Medicaid benefits within a very high quality long term care facility. Within the facility, it is not uncommon for the staff to be entirely unaware of who is on Medicaid and who is on "private pay." Indeed, in many cases, a private pay patient may end up sharing a room with a Medicaid patient, and the staff has no idea how each resident is paying for the care.

On the other hand, Medicaid does not pay for various services and items that make life more pleasurable for a long term care resident: a television, certain therapies, vitamins, outside recreation, transportation to outside events, trips to the beauty shop, extra food and snacks, etc. That is one reason it is such a good idea to have maintained a "safety net" through advance planning—so that resources will be available to pay for these niceties of life.

Can you get a private room on Medicaid?

Usually not, but if the doctor indicates that there is a solid medical reason why a private room is needed, the family can pay the difference and the client will be able to have a private room (if one is available). This is another reason that it is a good idea to have maintained a "safety net" through planning.

What Medicaid planning strategies are still effective?

The primary planning strategy attorneys have employed for years, transferring assets into a Medicaid qualified trust, still works. However, the penalties are calculated differently now, so the net effect is that you need to transfer the property into the trust well in advance of the date that either spouse (or a single person) needs to apply for Medicaid long term benefits.

If time is short, Medicaid planning can also involve the purchase of annuities, the granting of an interest in the family home to family members, and other techniques.

As indicated earlier, the laws and rules change constantly so it is not possible to be too specific on what sort of techniques might be used in any given situation, as a current technique might not apply to a certain situation, or might be prohibited by the time you read this book. However, the fundamental concept of Medicaid qualification planning is to transfer various assets into a special Medicaid qualified trust or into the names of trusted people, so that those assets will be available later as a form of "safety net"—or the income from those assets will be available later, as a form of "safety net income." Which transfers will work in any individual case will vary widely, which is why it is important to consult with a qualified attorney prior to commencing any transfers.

What sort of "penalties" are involved in Medicaid planning?

There are two kinds of penalties—real penalties and delay "penalties." The only way you can incur a real penalty (a fine or jail time) is to falsify an application or intentionally conceal and fail to disclose assets. Good attorneys will never do this, so their clients never face real penalties if they follow their attorney's advice.

The other "penalty" is simply a delay that is imposed by Medicaid before an applicant is granted benefits. For example, if it turned out that an applicant made a transfer of $10,000 that was not permitted under the rules at the time of transfer, Medicaid would impose a two month "penalty" on that applicant, which simply means that the applicant would not receive benefits for two months after he or she otherwise would be qualified. It is important to understand two things about these types of delay "penalties."

First, a transfer does not have to be underhanded in order to create a delay "penalty." For example, donations to your church are not permitted under the regulations. Therefore, if the applicant had been making $200 monthly tithes to his or her church all of his life, and if he or she finally ran out of assets and applied for Medicaid long term care benefits, Medicaid could look back for five years (60 months) and impose a delay "penalty" based upon impermissible transfers of $12,000 (60 months x $200), which would cause a delay "penalty" of about two and one-half months. In other words he or she would not be able to qualify for Medicaid long term care benefits for two and one-half months after the date he or she otherwise would be able to qualify. It is unknown whether Medicaid would actually impose the delay "penalty" in that case, but it clearly could do so under the new rules.

The second thing to understand is that a good Medicaid qualification planner takes these delay "penalties" into account, factors them into the plan, and ensures that there will be sufficient resources available to pay the nursing home bills, as well as the other household expenses, during the delay "penalty" period. The delay "penalty" is actually part of the plan.

Is it possible to preserve all of your assets and still qualify for Medicaid?

In theory, the answer is "yes," but it is a very qualified "yes." To protect all of your assets you would need to complete your planning more than five years in advance of when you need to apply for Medicaid, you need to make the transfers either to a trust or to very reliable people who would be willing to support you (remember, you gave away all of your assets), and you need to be very careful to observe all of the formalities. In addition, it would help if you had a very good, stable, source of income that meets all of your needs other than long term care.

The reality is that most people who put Medicaid qualification plans in place do not preserve all of their assets; they simply protect a significant portion of their assets in order to provide a "safety net" for themselves and their spouse. If one of them needs long term care, they end up paying some portion of their long term care bills out of their hard-earned savings.

Actually, the sad reality is that many people never plan, and if one of them needs long term care, they spend their entire savings on that care and end up totally impoverished. In that case, they become totally dependent upon the whims of the Medicaid caseworker and ever-changing government rules.

None of this sounds very attractive; isn't there anything else we can do?

Yes, there are some things everyone should do. First, everyone should at least investigate Long Term Care Insurance. Many people do not investigate Long Term Care Insurance until it is too late: they develop an illness or condition that makes them uninsurable, or simply reach an age where the insurance is no longer available. That is a shame, because Long Term Care Insurance very often is the best way to manage the risk that you will need long term care. There are a variety of products available today that reduce the premiums, or help take the sting out of paying the premiums for the policy, such as "return of premium" riders, which pay either you or your estate back all of the premiums you paid in if you never need long term care. There are also joint policies that allow two spouses to pay one premium and share the benefits, etc.

Many people initially believe that they cannot afford the premiums of a Long Term Care Insurance policy, but change their mind when they meet with a good insurance professional who understands how to design a Long Term Care Insurance policy for a client's specific needs. For example, you may decide to buy only a three-year-benefit policy. In that way, if you do eventually need long term care, your family can put a Medicaid qualification plan in place, the Long Term Care policy will pay the cost of the first three years of care, and you will only need to pay for two years of additional care (and possibly much less) out of your own assets before being able to qualify for Medicaid benefits.

If you investigate and find that you cannot qualify for Long Term Care Insurance, then that is a fairly good indication that you are at increased risk for needing long term care. If this is the case, you should consult with a qualified attorney as soon as possible to see what you can do under the laws and rules currently in effect to protect as many of your assets as possible and to create a "safety net."

Chapter 13

- Taxes -

Although taxes are only a small piece in the estate planning puzzle, a basic understanding of the fundamental tax rules can help to understand why your attorney is making specific recommendations for your estate plan. The purpose of this Chapter is not to advocate any particular estate planning strategy but to familiarize you with the fundamental tax rules that apply to all estates. Since all of the numbers, percentages and amounts indicated in this Chapter are subject to change at any time, you should consult with a qualified estate planning attorney at the time you plan to determine the current state of the law.

What are the types of taxes that are affected by my estate planning?

The taxes that come into play most prominently are the federal estate tax, the federal gift tax, and capital gains tax. Income taxes can also be an issue, particularly when you have significant amounts in your qualified retirement plans like an IRA or 401(k). The Chapter on IRAs and other qualified retirement plans (Chapter 15, Individual Retirement Accounts) addresses these taxes in more detail.

What assets are subject to estate tax?

The *federal estate tax* is a tax levied against any "right to control" property that the decedent had at the time of his or her death. For federal estate tax purposes, any assets owned or controlled by the decedent at the time of death are included in his or her estate. The decedent's debts, funeral costs, and estate administration expenses can be deducted from the value of the estate assets to calculate the value of the estate subject to tax.

Some assets are clearly understood to be part of one's estate, such as real estate or bank accounts one owns at the time of death. Yet the "right to control" concept includes some assets that many people do not generally consider part of their estate, such as life insurance. Although life insurance death proceeds are generally not subject to income tax, they are not automatically exempt from federal estate tax. The proceeds of any life insurance policy that is owned by the decedent or in which the decedent had any "incidents of ownership" at the time of death are included in the decedent's taxable estate. Incidents of ownership are a term of art. They include the ownership of the policy, power to change the beneficiary, right to borrow against the policy, and right to surrender or cancel the policy.

Because these incidents of ownership are key, it is less important whose life is the subject of the insurance. For example, a husband may own life insurance on his wife. Because the husband has the ability to change the beneficiary of the policy, borrow against it, and has other rights that come with being the owner, the policy will be taxed as part of the husband's estate. This can be especially counterintuitive when the husband dies before the wife, subjecting the estate to potential tax on an asset that may have little value until later, when the wife dies.

What is the federal gift tax?

As a general rule, there is a *federal gift tax* on gifts made during one's lifetime. The tax is assessed against the donor, and not the recipient. The tax applies regardless of whether the donor and the recipient are related.

There is a common misconception that the gift tax can be avoided if the recipient pays the donor a nominal sum for the property. However, a gift is made whenever property is transferred for less than its fair value. If a father transfers real estate worth $100,000 to his son in exchange for $10, the father has made a sale for $10 and a gift of the remaining $99,990.

Does Colorado have an estate or gift tax?

Under the current tax system in effect through 2012, Colorado does not have a tax on lifetime gifts or transfers at

death. If you own property in another state when you die, it
may be subject to estate or inheritance tax in that state, so it
is important to tell your attorney about all property that you
own.

Why does the system change in 2013?

The current federal estate and gift tax law is due to
"sunset" after December 31, 2012. This Chapter addresses
current tax law in effect until the end of 2012 (unless it is
changed prior to December 31, 2012). If you are reading this
AFTER 2012, please check our current website (found on the
back cover) for current information on any tax law changes.

What size estates are subject to estate or gift tax?

To understand when estate or gift taxes may be assessed,
imagine a coupon. Just like the coupons you may clip out of
the paper, this coupon is used to reduce the amount you
would otherwise have to pay. In this case, the payment you
are making is the combined estate and gift tax.

To continue the coupon analogy, imagine that all the
taxable gifts you make during your lifetime and all the assets
in your estate at death make up what is in your basket when
you go to pay for your purchases at the checkout counter.
(This system of combining the lifetime gifts and estate
transfers at death is why the federal gift and estate system
are considered "unified.") In a sense, every estate is subject
to estate and gift tax, just as every shopper has to go through

the checkout counter. But many taxpayers will be able to pay most or all of their tax with a "coupon." This coupon is a credit, technically called the applicable exclusion amount. As long as the total value of taxable gifts and taxable estate assets does not exceed the value of the coupon, no tax is due. If the total value of your "basket" exceeds the value of the coupon, you or your estate will have to pay tax on the difference between the amount in your basket and the amount of the coupon.

Now let's apply that coupon analogy to understand the gift and estate tax coupon system. In 2012, the coupon combined estate and gift taxes for those who die in those years is $5,120,000. So you can give away $1,000,000 of taxable gifts while you are alive and still have another $4,120,000 of coupon to apply to transfers from your estate when you die.

If you give away your entire coupon during your lifetime your estate will owe estate taxes. For example, if you give away taxable gifts that total $5,620,000, you will owe gift tax on the $500,000 difference between the total amount of taxable gifts and the $5,120,000 value of the gift tax "coupon." Your estate will have to pay estate tax on all the assets in your taxable estate because you have no coupon left. If you don't use any of your gift tax "coupon," then you can apply the entire amount of the "coupon," $5,120,000, to estate taxes at your death.

How does the coupon amount change after 2012?

Current law provides for the coupon to go down to $1,000,000 for gifts and deaths after 2012. This law is likely to change before 2013. Check our website (on the back cover) or confer with your attorney about the applicable coupon amounts in effect after 2012.

Are there any other exclusions from gift tax?

We've used the term "taxable gift" in this Chapter because some gifts will not even have to go through the checkout counter; that is, they won't be subject to federal gift tax regardless of the available coupon. The law calls these "de minimis" gifts but we call them "under the radar" gifts. This kind of gift is like flying "under the radar" because it does not count toward the coupon or credit discussed above. This "under the radar" treatment applies to an unlimited number of recipients per donor, and the donor and recipients need not be related. However, the exclusion considers the cumulative sum of all gifts made during the calendar year. For example, consider a year in which the "under the radar" amount is $13,000. If you make a $7,000 gift in February and a $7,000 gift in December to the same person, this would place $1,000 of your gifts above the radar and subject to gift tax (or use of $1,000 of your coupon). However, a $7,000 gift in December and a $7,000 gift the following January would both be under the radar because they were made in different calendar years. This $13,000 amount was the amount in 2012, but it changes over time based on inflation. Your attorney can advise you of the current amount for the year you are contemplating a major gift.

A common misconception is that smaller gifts for birthdays or other holidays do not count toward the "under the radar" exclusion. However, the exclusion considers all gifts made during the calendar year. Spouses can combine their "under the radar" gifts to give up to twice the exclusion amount in a year, even if the source of the gift comes from only one spouse. So a wife can give stock that was in her name only to her daughter. If the value of the stock is greater than the "under the radar" exclusion but less than twice the exclusion, the gift tax can be avoided; that is, the wife can avoid even having to use her gift tax coupon at the checkout counter, if the husband agrees to let the wife use some of his "under the radar" amount as well. To get even more bang for the buck, the wife can gift stock to both the daughter and the daughter's husband, thereby doubling the amount beyond what could have been given to the daughter alone.

Some gifts do not have to use the coupon or the "under the radar" exclusion. The payment of someone else's medical and educational expenses is completely exempt from gift tax. To avoid having to use the coupon or the "under the radar" exclusion, these payments must be made directly to the medical or educational provider.

What about gifts or estates between spouses?

If your spouse is a U.S. citizen, any transfer to him or her is eligible for the unlimited marital deduction. This exempts all gifts and estate transfers between spouses from any gift or estate tax. But it really is merely a deferral of these taxes because the spouse who receives all the assets must then pay gift or estate tax when transferring those assets to someone else. To explain, let's continue our "checkout counter" analogy. Let's use the example of a couple where the husband dies first. By using the marital deduction, all the assets in the husband's grocery basket are transferred to the wife's grocery basket *before* the husband reaches the checkout counter. Because the assets are now in the wife's basket, the husband won't have to pay anything at the checkout counter, and he won't use his coupon because there is nothing in his basket to pay for.

Sounds good, but remember that now the wife's basket contains both the husband's assets and the wife's assets. When the wife goes through the checkout counter of combined gift and estate taxes, she'll have to pay tax on all the assets combined. She can still use her own coupon to minimize the payment, but she may not be able to use her husband's coupon.

We say <u>may not</u> be able to use her husband's coupon because this is one of those laws that is set to change in 2013. For 2012, a surviving spouse can use the coupon of her deceased spouse (if she satisfies quite a few requirements). This is called "portability." But portability only applies to deaths of surviving spouses in 2011 and 2012 and it is set to expire when the law changes in 2013, so it should not be relied upon.

In 2013 and after, current law is as follows: Even though the husband didn't use his coupon because he used the marital deduction to avoid taxation on anything in his basket, the husband's coupon was personal to him alone, and cannot be used by the wife for her gift or estate tax. That is why tax planning must take into account what might happen upon the death of the second spouse, and cannot generally rely on the marital deduction alone to avoid taxes.

In addition, the martial deduction is not unlimited if your spouse is not a U.S. citizen. In that case, your attorney can recommend different estate planning techniques to minimize taxation on transfers to your spouse.

But my spouse and I together don't have enough in our estates to exceed our two coupons. Why do we need to plan for taxes?

The coupon amounts apply only to amounts that are not subject to the marital deduction, that is, transfers made to someone other than a spouse. As discussed in the question above, if you leave all your assets directly to your spouse, you may lose the opportunity to use your coupon while leaving your spouse with your combined assets and only one coupon.

Consider this example: Jerry leaves his entire estate of $500,000 to his wife Eleanor when Eleanor has her own assets of $1,000,000. Applying the marital deduction, there is no estate tax due at Jerry's death. In other words, Jerry avoided

the checkout counter by putting all his assets in Eleanor's
basket. However, when Eleanor dies, she'll have a combined
estate of $1,500,000. Assuming that at the time of Eleanor's
death the total coupon amount is $1,000,000 and there is no
portability between spouses, Eleanor's estate will pay tax on
$500,000.

How can a couple avoid "losing" the coupon on the estate of the first to die?

A common technique to utilize the coupons of **both**
spouses is the use of a trust. Consider Jerry and Eleanor from
the scenario above. Instead of leaving his estate to Eleanor,
Jerry leaves it to a testamentary trust, that is, a trust not
established until Jerry's death. This trust is designed to
benefit Eleanor and may have Eleanor serving as trustee to
manage the trust. Upon Jerry's death, all of Jerry's unused
"coupon" amount goes to this trust. In effect, by not leaving
it to Eleanor directly, Jerry went through the checkout
counter with his estate, and used his coupon to pay for all of
the amount in the trust. This trust will not be considered part
of Eleanor's estate because it is past the checkout counter and
moved out of the "tax store," so it will not be subject to estate
tax when Eleanor dies. This allows Eleanor to use and benefit
from Jerry's assets, without "losing" the coupon amount
available at Jerry's death.

If Jerry's estate is worth more than the available coupon,
the "excess" can go directly to Eleanor, or to a marital trust
that is designed to use the marital deduction. In both cases,

by using the marital deduction, Eleanor is able to defer the tax on that excess until she dies, but those "excess" assets will have to go through the "checkout counter" at the time of Eleanor's death along with all of the remaining assets that were originally Eleanor's even while Jerry was alive.

Are any other gifts exempt from taxation?

Gifts to qualified charities and political organizations are exempt from both gift and estate tax. See Chapter 10, Planning for Your Favorite Charities and Family Foundations, for more details on gifting to charities.

How much is the gift tax and estate tax?

This is an area of law that is likely to change in coming years. In 2012, the top rate of tax is 35%. If the law does not change, that rate will jump to 55% in 2013. Although the rates of tax on gifts and estates are the same, it can be more advantageous to make a lifetime gift than to plan for a transfer at death. For one thing, gifting during lifetime removes the value of the gift and any appreciation from your estate. In some instances, making a lifetime gift can remove both the value of the gift and the value of the gift tax from the estate, which can create an economic advantage.

Are there any other taxes we should consider in estate planning?

Your attorney can also help you minimize the capital

gains tax consequences of your estate plan. Capital gains taxes are income taxes imposed on the gain you recognize when you sell an asset. Gain is the difference between the sales price and your basis. Your basis is usually your cost to acquire the asset, often the purchase price. Understanding basis is important because when you gift an asset during your lifetime your basis "carries over" to the recipient. That is, the recipient's basis is the same as your basis was when you made the gift. In contrast, if you leave someone an asset when you die, the recipient's basis is generally the value of the asset at the time of your death.

An example can help explain the significance of this. Assume you purchase stock for $100 ("your basis"). If the stock is worth $200 when you give it away, the recipient has a basis in that stock of $100. If the recipient turns around and sells the stock for $200, the recipient will pay capital gains tax on the $100 difference between the sales price and the $100 basis. However, if you leave the same stock to the recipient at your death, the recipient's basis is the $200 value at the time of your death. Therefore, if the recipient sells the stock at that $200 price, the recipient will not pay any capital gains tax.

Considering capital gains consequences in planning your estate is important, but it must be considered in context. Currently, the top long-term capital gains rate is 15%, while the top estate tax rate is 35%. In addition, the capital gains tax only applies to the gain, while the estate tax applies to the entire value of the asset. Therefore, saving capital gains tax at the expense of estate tax savings can be counterproductive.

What is the Generation-skipping Transfer Tax?

This is a complex tax that was designed to keep wealthier taxpayers from transferring assets to lower generations—grandchildren for example—as a way to avoid estate taxes. The tax comes into play when a taxpayer skips at least one generation in making a transfer of property directly or within a will or trust. The GSTT may also apply to transfers of property to non-family members if the recipient is more than 37 ½ years younger than the person making the transfer. It is important to understand that the GSTT also has a "coupon" exemption amount that applies cumulatively to generation-skipping gifts made during life and at death, and that "coupon" can be leveraged through quality planning. Some ways to make a generation-skipping transfer without incurring unnecessary taxation are addressed in Chapters 16 and 17. Your attorney can recommend the best method for your situation.

Chapter 14

- Probate and Intestacy -

What is Probate?

Probate is the process whereby a court oversees and approves the transfer of assets of a dead person. Different states have different probate processes. Colorado's probate process can be easier than in some states, but what is easy in the eyes of an experienced estate attorney rarely seems as easy to the loved ones who are involved in the proceedings.

What happens when there is no will?

When there is no will, the decedent is said to have died "intestate." When that happens, the law provides its own rules that must be followed in probating the estate. These rules apply to the property of persons who are domiciled in the state of Colorado at the time of their death. Some of the common results of intestacy are described in this Chapter.

What assets are probated?

(a) Beneficiary assets

The probate process only applies to probate assets. To explain what a probate asset is, it helps to explain what is not a probate asset, and then to provide some examples. Non-probate assets include assets that transfer at death based on a beneficiary designation. Common examples of beneficiary-designated assets include life insurance, retirement plans, and some bank or brokerage accounts that are designated "payable on death" or "transfer on death."

Colorado is one of several states that allows for beneficiary deeds. Through the use of this deed, the owner of real property can designate one or more beneficiaries who will own the property upon the death of the original owner. A beneficiary deed can make real property that would otherwise be a probate asset a beneficiary asset. However, beneficiary deeds have some disadvantages. Property that is subject to a beneficiary deed will become a countable resource for the purposes of Medicaid qualification, even if the asset would not otherwise have been countable. The beneficiary designation may also make the beneficiary listed on the deed ineligible for Medicaid or other government-financed medical assistance. Also, if the beneficiary deed names several beneficiaries, all of the beneficiaries have some control over the property, leaving no one clearly "in charge" as there would be if there were a trustee of a trust or personal representative under a will in control of the property.

(b) Assets that transfer by virtue of law

Other assets that bypass probate are those that transfer automatically by process of law, such as assets held in joint tenancy or community property. Joint tenancy property is property that is held by multiple parties and the title or ownership document of the property clearly states that it is joint tenancy property. Upon the death of a joint tenant, ownership of the property automatically passes to the surviving joint tenant(s), and no probate is needed.

Community property is a form of property ownership between spouses only. Colorado is not a community property state, but Colorado law recognizes the community property status of property that was treated as community property in another state. Colorado law also recognizes the community property status of property that is acquired in Colorado with the direct proceeds of community property from another state. Like joint tenancy, community property passes automatically to the survivor upon the death of the one of the owners. There are tax implications to community property that should also be considered, so it is important to make your estate planning team aware of any community property you might have.

If an asset is held by more than one person and it is not specified as joint tenancy property, and it does not qualify as community property, then Colorado law will treat it as tenancy in common. Tenancy in common means that each owner owns his or her specified share of the property as a probate asset.

(c) Assets in Trust

Assets held in trust are also not probate assets. This means that if someone was the grantor or beneficiary of a trust, upon that person's death the property in the trust will transfer according to the terms of the trust without going through the probate process.

When we take away the non-probate assets that are beneficiary-designated assets, joint tenancy or community property assets, and trust assets, that leaves three types of assets as probate property: (1) assets owned in your own name only; (2) assets owned by you as a tenant in common; and (3) assets that would normally pass by beneficiary designation where there is no named beneficiary to receive the assets—these assets then are payable to the probate estate and are governed by the rules of the decedent's will or the laws of intestacy.

If I have a will, does that avoid probate?

No. The opposite is true. A will is a set of instructions about how you want your probate assets treated. Having a will means that you get to direct what happens to your probate assets, but they are still probate assets. Only changing the ownership of a probate asset to one of the types of non-probate assets will avoid probate.

How large does an estate have to be to require probate?

Any amount of real estate that is held as a probate asset must be probated. Most experienced estate planning attorneys have seen at least one case where resources were wasted to probate a small piece of real estate that may have cost more to probate than the property was worth.

For assets other than real estate, it may be possible to avoid probate if the probate estate is especially small. Under current law, if the total amount of probate assets is worth less than $50,000, a probate may be avoided and the assets collected through the use of an affidavit. However, where there are several heirs and they cannot work together on the collection of the assets and payment of the bills, a probate may still be necessary to put one person in charge to accomplish those things.

How does probate work?

Probate begins when someone interested in a dead person's estate opens a probate case with the court. The court then appoints a personal representative. The personal representative has the authority to collect the deceased person's probate property, pay the deceased person's debts, and transfer the probate property in accordance with the law. The actions of the personal representative are subject to the court's authority.

The court appoints the personal representative based on the wishes expressed in the deceased person's will. If there is no will, the personal representative is selected either by a majority of the deceased person's heirs, or from a list of people provided in the law. For example, a surviving spouse has priority under the law to be named personal representative. If there is no surviving spouse, all of the adult children of the deceased person have equal priority. If a majority of the heirs cannot decide among themselves which of the children should be personal representative, then the court will decide for them.

How long does probate take?

A common frustration with the probate process is the waiting period that must take place before the process can be completed. This period, which is generally at least one year, is designed to provide time for all creditors of the deceased person to come forward and make a claim against the estate. Avoiding probate does not mean that you can avoid paying the deceased person's creditors, but it can mean that you can speed up the process where you are confident that all of the bills have been paid and no other creditors will be making a claim. In other words, avoiding probate can allow your estate to be settled based on a timetable that fits the circumstances instead of a timetable mandated by the law.

Is the probate process private?

Probably not. All court cases are public records. While some Colorado courts may have court-specific policies to seal some probate cases from public review, this is in response to some concerns about identity theft that will probably be resolved in favor of renewed public access. The general policy is to make all records in the probate court available to the public.

What about probating property out of state?

A Colorado probate court usually does not have any authority over real estate located outside of Colorado. As a result, if the real estate is a probate asset, two probates will be required. A Colorado probate will be necessary because Colorado was the deceased person's residence at the time of death, and another type of probate will be required in the state where the real estate is located to probate the asset there. This is one reason many attorneys recommend the use of a living trust when there is real estate located out of state.

If there is no will, does the state get the property?

No. This is almost never the case. The laws of intestacy provide that someone related to the deceased person will inherit property where there is no will. The only time the government obtains a deceased person's assets is when no relatives can be found.

When there is no will, who inherits?

That depends on who are the nearest relatives of the deceased person. If the decedent was married at the time of death, the laws of intestacy provide that the surviving spouse is entitled to a portion of the estate. The size of that portion depends on whether there are any surviving descendants of the decedent, and the relationship of those descendants to the surviving spouse. For example, if there are children or grandchildren who are not the surviving spouse's children or grandchildren, then a portion of the estate may go to the children or grandchildren and another portion to the spouse.

If the deceased person left behind minor children, intestacy can leave a lot of decisions about the children in the hands of a judge. One decision is the choice of a guardian to make legal decisions about the child's care. Without a will or other writing in which the parent names a guardian, a judge must choose the guardian, based on the petition of any person who indicates an interest in the child's welfare.

Also, when a minor child inherits a parent's estate or non-probate assets, the child cannot own the property on his or her own. Therefore, an adult must be named to manage the child's assets until the child reaches the age of 21. If there is no will, the court will appoint a conservator to manage the child's money under court supervision until the child reaches the age of 21. Where one parent dies with a minor child, the court must then give priority to appointing the child's other parent as conservator of the child's inherited assets. When the parents were divorced, this may not be a desired result. Consider a man who divorced while his children were minors. Assume he dies while the children are still minors. Whether or not he had custody of the children after the divorce, the children's mother will be given first priority when the court names a conservator to manage the property the children inherited from their father. This may or may not have been the father's wishes, but without a will or trust for the father, it will usually be the result.

If the deceased person was not married and had no descendants, his or her surviving parent or parents will inherit, or the surviving siblings will inherit if there are no surviving parents.

Chapter 15

- Individual Retirement Accounts -

Historically, a personal residence was the largest asset in a person's estate. Currently, however, because of changes in tax laws and the tremendous historical growth of the equity markets, qualified retirement plans occupy a significant portion of many estates. The rise in the value of the assets held in qualified retirement plans has created new problems and opportunities. In most cases, qualified retirement plans subject the owner, their heirs or their estate to income tax liability, as well as potential estate tax liability. Although there are many different types of retirement plans, this Chapter deals with traditional IRAs and Rollover IRAs, generically "IRAs." Other plans, such as 401-k plans, 403-B plans and other tax-preferred plans (planners usually call these "qualified plans") usually have similar, if not identical treatment, and raise similar issues.

Why do I need to plan specifically, for my IRA as part of my estate plan?

More and more people are holding the bulk of their wealth in qualified plans and IRAs. With proper planning, participants can make the most of this income tax benefit and pass some of that benefit on to their beneficiaries as well as reduce the amount of estate tax that may be due. IRAs are unique in their tax treatment and may be subject to both income tax and estate tax. These taxes combined could subject the assets of your IRA to a total tax of 70% to 80%.

What do you mean my IRA is subject to both income tax and estate tax?

Your IRA is an asset you own at your death and it is therefore included in your estate for federal estate tax purposes and thus, if your estate is over the "coupon amount" (see Chapter 13), your IRA will be subject to estate tax. Any distributions from your IRA are also included in the gross income of the recipient in the year of the distribution.

When can I make withdrawals from my IRA?

You may withdraw assets from your IRA at any time. The purpose of an IRA is a savings vehicle for retirement; therefore, the IRS imposes penalties on withdrawals made too soon. If you withdraw assets from your IRA before reaching age 59 1/2, you will have to pay a 10% penalty tax *in addition* to the payment of ordinary income tax on the withdrawal (unless one of several limited exceptions applies).

Do I ever have to make withdrawals from my IRA?

As noted, if you make withdrawals too early you may be subject to the 10% penalty tax. You are also subject to a penalty tax if you fail to withdraw enough assets (the "Required Minimum Distribution") each year after you reach the "Required Beginning Date." The Required

Beginning Date, is generally April 1 of the year after the year in which you reach age 70 ½. For every year after the year in which you reach age 70 ½, you must withdraw your Required Minimum Distribution by December 31 of that year. If you do not withdraw at least the Required Minimum Distribution by the Required Beginning Date, a 50% penalty tax is imposed on the amount that should have been withdrawn but wasn't, in addition to the ordinary income tax on the distribution. This Required Minimum Distribution also applies in the year of your death.

How is the Required Minimum Distribution computed?

The Required Minimum Distribution is determined actuarially; basically, you divide the amount of assets held in the IRA in any given year by your remaining life expectancy. Your life expectancy is obtained from the IRS Uniform Lifetime Tables (see the next page). Each year you will look to the tables, find your age, and use the Applicable Divisor listed for your age. You then divide the value of the assets in the IRA as of December 31 of the previous year to determine you Required Minimum Distribution for the current year.

There is an exception to the calculation above if your spouse is more than ten years younger than you. In that case you would use a different table than the "Uniform Lifetime Table" on the next page, instead you would use the "IRS Joint and Last Survivor Table." The rest of the calculation remains the same.

Uniform Lifetime Table

For Use by:

- Unmarried Owners,
- Married Owners Whose Spouses Are Not More Than 10 Years Younger, and
- Married Owners Whose Spouses Are Not the Sole Beneficiaries of their IRAs

Age	Distribution Period	Age	Distribution Period
70	27.4	93	9.6
71	26.5	94	9.1
72	25.6	95	8.6
73	24.7	96	8.1
74	23.8	97	7.6
75	22.9	98	7.1
76	22.0	99	6.7
77	21.2	100	6.3
78	20.3	101	5.9
79	19.5	102	5.5
80	18.7	103	5.2
81	17.9	104	4.9
82	17.1	105	4.5
83	16.3	106	4.2
84	15.5	107	3.9
85	14.8	108	3.7
86	14.1	109	3.4
87	13.4	110	3.1
88	12.7	111	2.9
89	12.0	112	2.6
90	11.4	113	2.4
91	10.8	114	2.1
92	10.2	115 and over	1.9

Can you give an example?

Assume that Mr. Smith just turned age 70 1/2 , and thus will be considered age 70 under IRS rules. Also assume that Mr. Smith's IRA had a balance of $1,000,000 on December 31 of last year. To determine the amount that Mr. Smith must withdraw to avoid penalties, you simply divide the balance of his IRA at the end of the prior year by the number of years indicated under the table above. For the first year, divide the balance by 27.4. For the second year, you divide the balance by 26.5, and so on, as the IRS Uniform Lifetime Table provides. As an example, assume Mr. Smith's IRA had a balance of $1,000,000 in the first year. You divide $1,000,000 by 27.4 and find that he must withdraw $37,736 before December 31 of that year.

What if the Required Minimum Distribution is not enough to cover my expenses?

You can always withdraw more than the Required Minimum Distribution. However, anything withdrawn in excess of the Required Minimum Distribution can not be used to offset future years' Required Minimum Distributions. As with all distributions from the IRA, the distribution is taxable income in the year withdrawn. The Required Minimum Distribution is the minimum you must withdraw to avoid the 50% penalty tax, not a maximum; you are always free to withdraw more than the minimum amount.

What if I own more than one IRA?

You must compute the Required Minimum Distribution

for each IRA, and then add all Required Minimum Distributions together. You then have the option to withdraw the total of all the Required Minimum Distributions, in equal or unequal installments, from any one or more of your IRAs to the complete exclusion of others.

What happens to my IRA after my death?

After your death, all of the assets in the IRA belong to the beneficiaries of the IRA. The beneficiary usually has options as to how they withdraw the assets. As discussed above, any distribution from the IRA is income taxable to the recipient in the year of receipt. A beneficiary may withdraw all of the assets at once, or may "stretch out" (described below) the distributions by withdrawing only the Required Minimum Distribution. If the spouse is the beneficiary, the spouse may "rollover" the IRA into his or her own IRA subject to all the rules discussed above, or keep the IRA in your name and withdraw the Required Minimum Distribution. If you are at least age 70 ½ at the time of your death, and if you have not withdrawn the Required Minimum Distribution for that year, then your beneficiaries will be required to take that distribution by December 31 of that year and the distribution will be fully income taxable to the recipient.

What is a "Rollover" IRA?

A rollover IRA is an IRA that your surviving spouse has inherited from you and rolled over into his or her own IRA or a new IRA in your surviving spouse's name. Once the IRA has been rolled over, your spouse owns the assets of the IRA, has complete control of the assets, and is free to dispose of those assets as he or she sees fit. The surviving spouse is the only person that has that option; any other beneficiary that inherits your IRA will have an inherited IRA.

What is an inherited IRA?

An inherited IRA is an IRA that remains in your name after your death for the benefit of the beneficiaries. This ability to leave the IRA in a tax deferred environment creates the opportunity for a significant amount of wealth to be generated without being subject to income taxation on an annual basis.

What is a "Stretch Out" IRA?

Assuming that your beneficiary is younger than you, the term "stretch out" describes the ability for your beneficiary to withdraw the IRA assets over his or her life expectancy, based on the table below, rather than your remaining hypothetical life expectancy. The beneficiary will still have a Required Minimum Distribution to withdraw each year, but if he or she uses his or her life expectancy rather than your life expectancy, that Required Minimum Distribution will be less each year, allowing the assets in the IRA to continue to grow tax deferred. For example, assume Mr. Smith died this year at age 75. Also assume Mr. Smith named his son, Joe, age 45, as the beneficiary of his IRA. Joe is now going to be required to take Required Minimum Distributions. If Joe does not stretch out the IRA, he will be required to use Mr. Smith's theoretical life expectancy from the table below, which is 13.4 years and Joe will be required to withdraw the remaining assets in the IRA over the next 13.4 years. If Joe stretches out the IRA, he will be allowed to use his life expectancy from the table below, which is 38.8 years. Now Joe will be able to withdraw the remaining IRA assets over 38.8 years.

Single Life Expectancy

For Use by Beneficiaries

Age	Life Expectancy	Age	Life Expectancy
0	82.4	28	55.3
1	81.6	29	54.3
2	80.6	30	53.3
3	79.7	31	52.4
4	78.7	32	51.4
5	77.7	33	50.4
6	76.7	34	49.4
7	75.8	35	48.5
8	74.8	36	47.5
9	73.8	37	46.5
10	72.8	38	45.6
11	71.8	39	44.6
12	70.8	40	43.6
13	69.9	41	42.7
14	68.9	42	41.7
15	67.9	43	40.7
16	66.9	44	39.8
17	66.0	45	38.8
18	65.0	46	37.9
19	64.0	47	37.0
20	63.0	48	36.0
21	62.1	49	35.1
22	61.1	50	34.2
23	60.1	51	33.3
24	59.1	52	32.3
25	58.2	53	31.4
26	57.2	54	30.5
27	56.2	55	29.6

Single Life Expectancy Continued

For Use by Beneficiaries

Age	Life Expectancy	Age	Life Expectancy
56	28.7	84	8.1
57	27.9	85	7.6
58	27.0	86	7.1
59	26.1	87	6.7
60	25.2	88	6.3
61	24.4	89	5.9
62	23.5	90	5.5
63	22.7	91	5.2
64	21.8	92	4.9
65	21.0	93	4.6
66	20.2	94	4.3
67	19.4	95	4.1
68	18.6	96	3.8
69	17.8	97	3.6
70	17.0	98	3.4
71	16.3	99	3.1
72	15.5	100	2.9
73	14.8	101	2.7
74	14.1	102	2.5
75	13.4	103	2.3
76	12.7	104	2.1
77	12.1	105	1.9
78	11.4	106	1.7
79	10.8	107	1.5
80	10.2	108	1.4
81	9.7	109	1.2
82	9.1	110	1.1
83	8.6	111 and over	1.0

Does it matter what age I am at my death?

There are different rules that apply if you die before the Required Beginning Date than if you die after the Required

Beginning Date. However, if the beneficiaries are all "Designated Beneficiaries," then the beneficiaries may "stretch out" the distributions over their life expectancy. If you die before the Required Beginning Date and all of the beneficiaries are not Designated Beneficiaries, then the assets must be withdrawn within five years. If you die after the Required Beginning Date and all of the beneficiaries are not Designated Beneficiaries, then the assets must be withdrawn over your hypothetical remaining life expectancy, according to the IRS tables.

What is a Designated Beneficiary?

The term "designated beneficiary" means an individual who has been designated either by the terms of the IRA plan or by the owner of the IRA. A simple way to remember is: does the beneficiary have a heartbeat? If the beneficiary has a heartbeat the beneficiary is, generally, a designated beneficiary. A trust, though not an individual, can qualify as a designated beneficiary if certain rules are complied with.

When do my beneficiaries have to start making distributions?

If the beneficiary is your spouse, your spouse may "rollover" your IRA into his or her own IRA and all of the rules discussed above apply. If the beneficiary is someone other than your spouse, the beneficiary must begin withdrawing Required Minimum Distributions in the year following your death.

In the case where your surviving spouse is younger than 59 ½ and has a need to access the IRA assets, performing a spousal rollover/election will preclude the surviving spouse from accessing the account without incurring a 10% penalty tax for early distributions. However, if the surviving spouse were to leave the IRA in your name (as an "inherited IRA"), your spouse may begin taking Required Minimum Distributions in the year following your death.

If my spouse elects to rollover my IRA into his or her IRA, who are the beneficiaries after my spouse dies?

Once your spouse elects to rollover the IRA, then the IRA belongs to your spouse and the beneficiaries are the persons he or she designates. If your spouse fails to designate a beneficiary, then the beneficiaries are whoever the IRA plan agreement lists as default beneficiaries.

Can my revocable living trust be named as a beneficiary of my IRA?

A trust can be named as a beneficiary of your IRA. If the trust does not meet the test for a Designated Beneficiary, then the trust will be required to withdraw the IRA assets within a five year period. If the trust meets the Designated Beneficiary test, then the trust can stretch out the IRA as described above. You should work with a qualified estate planner to make sure your trust will qualify as a Designated Beneficiary.

Why would I name my revocable living trust as a beneficiary of my IRA?

Naming the trust as a beneficiary gives the estate planner greater flexibility for post-death planning. It can also afford your beneficiaries some protections that they may not be able to provide for themselves. Moreover, it may give you the opportunity to use your federal estate tax exemption when you may not have enough other assets to do so otherwise and thus limit or eliminate potential estate taxes.

What do you mean my IRA could use my federal estate tax exemption?

Assume Mr. Smith owns an IRA with $1,500,000 in assets and Mrs. Smith also owns other property with a value of $1,500,000. If Mr. Smith names Mrs. Smith as the beneficiary of his IRA, at his death, Mrs. Smith will then own her own property of $1,500,000 and Mr. Smith's IRA of $1,500,000. If Mrs. Smith dies shortly thereafter, she will have a taxable estate of $3,000,000. Assuming, for example, that the federal estate tax exemption at that time is $2,000,000 per individual, Mrs. Smith's estate would be subject to federal estate tax on $1,000,000. If Mr. Smith had named a trust as beneficiary, we would have been able to utilize Mr. Smith's federal estate tax exemption (or "coupon;" see Chapter 13, Taxes) and neither Mr. Smith nor Mrs. Smith would have been subject to the federal estate tax.

Chapter 16

- Protecting Future Generations ~ Dynasty Trusts -

What is a Dynasty Trust?

A dynasty trust is one established and funded by a trustmaker and designed to last for many generations. The trust is designed to pay income and principal to various generations of beneficiaries based upon specific criteria set forth in the trust by the trustmaker. Distributions could be quite broad, for example for the health, education and maintenance of each generation, or distributions could be quite restricted, for example only to be used to provide each generation with a college education. In addition to rewarding certain behavior, the terms of the dynasty trust could also be designed to discourage certain behavior, such as smoking, divorce, or illegal drug use.

The concept of the dynasty trust is that the funds would escape gift, estate and generation-skipping transfer tax when contributed to the trust, and would continue to avoid such taxes for generation after generation as long as the dynasty trust lasted. Funds contributed to the dynasty trust may (or may not) be subject to gift or estate taxes when they are contributed to the dynasty trust, but will thereafter be outside of the estate, gift and generation-skipping transfer tax system—forever. Income taxes, of course, will be due as the income is earned and realized by the dynasty trust.

How does a Dynasty Trust work?

Typically, a dynasty trust will be established by a trustmaker at death. A dynasty trust can be established during life, but the amount contributed to the dynasty trust may be subject to gift tax to the extent it exceeds the lifetime gift tax exemption. The generation-skipping tax system is separate from and in addition to the estate and gift tax system. As a consequence, both tax systems need to be kept in mind when designing dynasty trusts.

If the dynasty trust is established at the death of the trustmaker, an amount equal to the maximum generation-skipping transfer tax exemption is placed in the dynasty trust. No tax will be due on this transfer. The proceeds are held in the trust and invested and administered for the benefit of subsequent generations. The initial beneficiaries of the dynasty trust could be the children of the trustmaker, the grandchildren, or subsequent generations. Depending on how the trust is designed, it would continue to make income and/or principal distributions to or for the benefit of each generation for as long as the trustmaker desires, or until the trust runs out of money. The dynasty trust could potentially last forever in those few states that that have entirely eliminated the "rule against perpetuities." Colorado permits a trust to last 1,000 years, but many states still prohibits a trust from lasting more than 90 years. Therefore, it is important to create a dynasty trust in a state such as Colorado. This ability to last forever (or at least 1,000 years) gives the dynasty trust its name. This means that the trust can last as long as there are future generations to receive distributions from the dynasty trust.

What is Generation-skipping Transfer Tax?

The generation-skipping transfer tax is an attempt by Congress to tax transfers of wealth that skip over one or more generations. Prior to the creation of the generation-skipping transfer tax by Congress, trustmakers would very often establish a trust for the benefit of their children that would be available to the children for their lifetimes. At the death of the children, the grandchildren would then become the beneficiaries. Because the children did not have total use and control of the trust assets, those funds were allowed to move from the children's generation to the grandchildren's generation without any estate tax whatsoever. In fact, this arrangement could last forever.

As a result of what the IRS perceived as the loss of estate tax revenue from the assets held in these early dynasty trusts, the IRS appealed to Congress to create and impose a tax at each generation. Congress adopted the IRS position only in part. Congress no longer allowed unlimited amounts of wealth to be placed in a dynasty trust, but did permit an amount up to the "generation-skipping tax exclusion amount" to continue to be placed in a dynasty trust. Over time this "generation-skipping tax exclusion amount" has risen significantly, which now allows savvy trustmakers to create very meaningful dynasty trusts.

If the trust is carefully created and no more that the applicable generation-skipping tax exclusion amount is transferred to the trust, the contributed property may remain in the trust and appreciate far in excess of the initial contribution. This means that as the trust grows and benefits subsequent generations, there will be no further transfer tax (i.e., no gift tax, no estate tax, no generation-skipping transfer tax) imposed on any distributions from the dynasty trust.

When would I want to use a Dynasty Trust?

The use of the dynasty trust found its beginnings as a technique to remove a certain portion of a trustmaker's wealth, plus all of the growth of that wealth, from the gift and estate tax system permanently (or at least for 1,000 years). It still provides that benefit, but only if the trust is properly and carefully designed as a dynasty trust.

Informed readers know that Congress constantly tinkers with the transfer tax system, increasing and decreasing the gift and estate tax exemptions, raising and lowering the gift and estate tax rates, etc. That is the attraction of the dynasty trust to savvy trustmakers: regardless of what Congress does in the future, it is likely that we will still have some form of gift and estate taxes and the dynasty trust will continue to be useful in moving assets entirely outside of the gift and estate tax system.

There are also many non-tax reasons for creating a dynasty trust, which greatly increase its value as a planning tool. The importance of these non-tax reasons will vary depending upon the needs and desires of the trustmaker. Dynasty trusts can be created to provide extremely solid creditor and predator protection for the beneficiaries of the trust, for generation after generation. The dynasty trust can also provide a pool of assets to be managed by a trustee for the benefit of all of the beneficiaries. This can prevent individual beneficiaries from squandering their inheritance by misusing the funds or investing inappropriately, thereby depriving the trustmaker's other descendants from the opportunities that could flow from the trustmaker's wealth. In addition, the dynasty trust can be established for certain specific purposes that are important to the trustmaker, such as the education of his or her descendants for generations to come. The dynasty trust can also be used to encourage participation in certain worthwhile causes, to discourage behavior that is unacceptable, or to provide a shield against divorce proceedings initiated against a beneficiary of the trust or against creditors of a beneficiary arising out of a business failure or mismanagement of money. These are just some of the many non-tax reasons a trustmaker might want to use a dynasty trust, and your attorney can help you determine if a dynasty trust will help you realize your Legacy planning goals.

Can I use a Dynasty Trust in conjunction with my irrevocable life insurance trust?

The answer is yes. An irrevocable life insurance trust (ILIT) can be drafted to include dynasty trust provisions, resulting in a very powerful tool that provides great leverage for the use of the generation-skipping tax exemption. (See Chapter 17 regarding ILITs.) In general, upon creation of the dynasty ILIT, money is contributed to the trust by the trustmaker and the trust uses that money to purchase life insurance on the life of the trustmaker. The funds contributed to the ILIT can qualify for the generation-skipping tax exemption, thus creating a dynasty ILIT. If done properly, upon the death of the insured, the life insurance death benefit flows into the dynasty ILIT and no estate or gift taxes are paid on the insurance death proceeds for generations. The use of life insurance in conjunction with a dynasty trust can provide great leverage in the use of the generation-skipping exclusion amount as well as provide great benefit to multiple generations.

Chapter 17

- Irrevocable Life Insurance Trusts -

Are life insurance proceeds (death benefit) taxable?

Generally, the death benefit of a life insurance policy is not subject to income taxes. However, the death benefit is subject to estate taxes at the death of the insured if the insured had any control of the policy. If the insured was the owner of the insurance policy, had the ability to change the beneficiary of the insurance policy, or could borrow against the cash surrender value of the insurance policy, the death benefit will be subject to estate taxes at the insured's death.

What is an irrevocable life insurance trust?

It is a trust designed to own and be the beneficiary of a life insurance policy on the life of the trustmaker. The proceeds of the life insurance policy, following the death of the trustmaker, are held, invested, and distributed according to the terms of the irrevocable life insurance trust (ILIT). The trust can be designed to:

- distribute those proceeds outright to the beneficiary or beneficiaries, or
- hold the proceeds for the benefit of the beneficiary or beneficiaries.

The proceeds, if held for the benefit of the beneficiary, can be distributed later upon the beneficiary attaining certain ages, such as one-third at 25 years of age; one-half of the balance at 30 years of age; and the balance at 35 years of age. The ILIT can be designed to distribute the proceeds upon the occurrence of any milestone or event, such as completing college or marriage.

The trust can also hold the life insurance proceeds for the entire life of the beneficiary, investing the proceeds and making distributions from the ILIT to the beneficiary for his or her health, education, maintenance, support and welfare. The possibilities available for the beneficiary are the same as for any other trust, including dynasty trust provisions (see Chapter 16, Protecting Future Generations ~ Dynasty Trusts).

Typically, a prospective insured will create an ILIT to own and be the beneficiary of a life insurance policy on the life of the trustmaker (insured). The terms of the trust may provide that at the trustmaker/insured's death, the death proceeds of the life insurance policy may be used to pay debts and taxes of the trustmaker/insured, with the balance held for the benefit of the trustmaker/insured's spouse and/ or children.

What is the purpose of an ILIT?
The ILIT is designed to own and collect the proceeds of a life insurance policy. The reason for putting the life insurance in the ILIT is two-fold. The first is to remove the life insurance proceeds from the estate of the insured, thus, avoiding estate taxes on the death benefit. The second is to place the cash value of the life insurance policy and the death benefit beyond the reach of lawsuits and claims against the insured.

For those with estates in excess of the amount of the estate tax exclusion, and for those whose estates would exceed the amount of the estate tax exclusion if the life insurance proceeds were included in the estate, the ILIT offers a very effective planning technique. If the ILIT owns the insurance policy on the life of the insured, and the formalities of the ILIT are followed, the value of the ILIT is not included in the insured's estate. Thus, the insurance death proceeds are not subject to estate tax, yet the death proceeds are available to pay the estate tax of the insured's estate or any other obligations of the insured.

If the purpose of the insurance is to replace the income that would be lost upon the death of the insured, the ILIT provides a viable tool to fully protect those funds. By placing the death proceeds in a properly designed ILIT, the proceeds can be placed out of the reach of a beneficiary's creditors. In this way, if the beneficiary is sued, suffers a business failure, or is the cause of a terrible accident for which the beneficiary is responsible, the funds held by the ILIT are protected from those creditors, yet can be used to provide for all of the beneficiary's needs. If the beneficiary is married or might marry someday, the insurance proceeds can be protected from the spouse of the beneficiary in the event of divorce or upon the death of the beneficiary.

If the purpose of the insurance is to build wealth, the same protections can be designed into the ILIT. The difficulty with using an ILIT for wealth replacement is that access is limited. Wealth replacement ILITs are most often used in conjunction with charitable remainder trusts to replace the amount passing to the charity at the end of the term of the charitable remainder trust. (See Chapter 10, Planning for your Favorite Charities and Family Foundations.) A charitable remainder trust offers great advantage to the trustmaker, but at the end of its term, usually the life of the trustmaker, the trust proceeds pass to a charity. This effectively disinherits the trustmaker's beneficiaries. By purchasing a life insurance policy on the life of the trustmaker in an ILIT in an amount equal to the value of the property passing to the charity at the end of the term of the charitable remainder trust, a trustmaker can replace the funds going to charity and pass them on to the beneficiaries estate tax free.

How does an ILIT work?

The steps to successfully establishing an ILIT are the following:

1. Design and create the ILIT.
2. The trustee of the ILIT applies for insurance.
3. The trustmaker contributes the premium to the ILIT.
4. The trustee notifies the beneficiaries of their demand right (described below).
5. The trustee pays the premium for the insurance.

The design of the ILIT will depend upon the purpose of the ILIT. An ILIT doesn't exist until it is created. The ILIT must be in existence and a trustee must be named at the time the life insurance policy application is submitted to the insurance company.

The trustee of the ILIT must apply for the insurance on the life of the insured. This is critical to the successful establishment of the ILIT. If the insured applies for the insurance policy, the death benefit may be subject to estate taxes at the death of the insured. This is especially true if the insured dies within the first three years of the policy.

The ILIT typically doesn't own any other assets, other than the insurance policy. As a consequence, the insured trustmaker will have to contribute money to the ILIT so that the trustee can pay the insurance premiums. After the trustee receives the premium, he or she notifies the beneficiaries that they have 30 days in which to exercise their right of withdrawal (a "demand right"). The right of withdrawal is necessary to avoid the taxation of the contribution to the ILIT as a taxable gift. Each person can give a present interest gift of a certain amount each year to any number of beneficiaries without the gifts being subject to gift tax. In 2012 that amount is $13,000, and is indexed for inflation, which is called the annual gift tax exclusion (see Chapter 13, Taxes). In order to qualify for the annual gift tax exclusion, the gift must be one of a present interest, not a future interest. Only gifts that the recipient has the right to the present use and enjoyment of are present interest gifts. The problem is that gifts to a trust are future interest gifts, not present interest gifts, and thus do not qualify for the annual gift tax exclusion. That is, the beneficiaries do not normally have a right to the present use of the contributions to the trust. They will receive the trust proceeds some time in the future, but generally have no present right to the trust assets. However, if the ILIT gives the beneficiaries the right to withdraw those funds for 30 days, they are then entitled to the present use and enjoyment for that 30 day period. That right is enough to cause what is otherwise a future interest gift to be a present interest gift. This right of withdrawal technique is sometimes called a Crummey right, named after the court decision that confirmed the effective use of this technique.

If the beneficiaries do not exercise their right of withdrawal within the 30 days, this right expires and the trustee is then free to pay the life insurance premium.

Why would I want an ILIT?

The reason for establishing an ILIT may be to provide funds to pay estate taxes or debts due upon the death of the insured. If the insured were to own the policy individually, it would be included in the insured's estate for estate tax purposes and might, if the estate is not already subject to estate taxes, cause the estate to be subject to estate taxes as a result of the inclusion of the death benefit in the insured's estate. Placing the life insurance policy inside of the ILIT removes the death benefit from the estate of the decedent, thus escaping estate tax and avoiding creditor claims.

Another reason for using an ILIT would be to protect the life insurance cash surrender value from the creditors of the insured. If the life insurance is held by an ILIT, it can be designed in a way to place the insurance death benefit and also the cash surrender value of the insurance policy out of the reach of the insured's creditors.

One might also use an ILIT to control the life insurance death proceeds after they are paid out and available to the beneficiaries of the trust. If the death proceeds were payable directly to a beneficiary, not only would they be subject to the claims of the beneficiary's creditors and predators, they would also be at the beneficiary's full disposal. If death proceeds are placed in an ILIT, the trustmaker can place certain restrictions and protections on the use of the death proceeds by the beneficiaries.

What are some other uses of an ILIT?

ILITs can be used in conjunction with buy-sell agreements to protect the ownership of a business in the event of the death of the owner. The insurance on the life of the business owner is owned by the ILIT. At the owner's death, the ILIT purchases his or her ownership interest in the business with the life insurance death proceeds received from the insurance company.

An ILIT can be used by business owners to equalize their estates between children who are active in the business and children who are not active in the business. The ILIT is one way to make sure that the business is passed to those children who have been active in the business and have demonstrated a desire to own the business, and yet distribute an equal amount of cash to the other children who are not active in the business. The ILIT makes the equal division of the business owner's estate among all of his or her children possible.

Similarly, an ILIT can be used to provide for children of a first marriage, leaving the balance of the estate to the surviving spouse. This minimizes conflict and the potential for resentment between the surviving spouse and the children from a prior marriage. (See Chapter 6, Blended Families and Second Marriages.)

Wealth replacement is another use for ILITs. Wealth replacement ILITs are most often used in conjunction with a charitable remainder trust. Upon creation of a charitable remainder trust, the trustmaker contributes property to the trust. The property placed in the charitable remainder trust is often sold shortly after its contribution. Because the charitable remainder trust is a charity, for tax law purposes, the trustmaker receives an income tax deduction for a portion of the value of the property contributed to the charitable remainder trust, and the proceeds from the sale of the contributed property are not subject to income or capital gain tax. As a result, the full proceeds of the sale, without reduction for income taxes, are invested by the trustee of the charitable remainder trust. The trustee of the charitable remainder trust distributes income to the trustmaker on at least an annual basis for the remainder of the life of the trustmaker. At the trustmaker's death, the remaining balance of the charitable remainder trust passes to a charity, thus disinheriting the trustmaker's children. An ILIT can be put in place that holds life insurance on the trustmaker's life. At the trustmaker's death, the insurance company would pay the death proceeds to the ILIT, which in turn would be used to replace the amounts that are going to the charity under the charitable remainder trust.

What if I want to access the cash value?

Generally speaking, the insured cannot directly access the cash value of an insurance policy owned by an ILIT. However, if the trust document permits, the insured can borrow funds from the life insurance trust, provided it is fully documented, interest is paid at the applicable rate, and the loan is repaid over time. ILITs can also be designed to provide access to the cash value of the life insurance policy by a spouse or a child of the insured. That type of ILIT is designed to allow for distributions to the spouse or the children.

Can I put something other than life insurance in the trust?

Yes. Any asset can be placed in the ILIT. Sometimes an income producing asset is placed inside of an ILIT to provide an income stream from which to pay the premiums on the life insurance. This technique eliminates any further contributions by the trustmaker/insured to the ILIT for the purpose of paying the life insurance premiums.

What happens to the ILIT when I die?

At the death of the insured, the insurance company pays the death proceeds to the ILIT. When the trustee of the ILIT receives those funds he must invest and administer them under the terms of the ILIT. The trustee can use those funds to pay debts and claims of the estate or to pay estate taxes. In most cases, those funds cannot be paid directly to the creditor; nor can they be paid to the IRS in satisfaction of estate taxes. To do so would cause those proceeds to be taxable in the estate of the insured trustmaker. One of the ways to avoid this result is to include a provision in the ILIT that it may loan the estate of the insured such amounts as are necessary to pay the estate tax or other debts or claims. The ILIT could also purchase property at full market value from the probate estate of the insured, and the proceeds received by the probate estate could be used to satisfy debts or to pay estate tax. The ILIT, when used for this purpose, and the estate plan should be coordinated to allow for the smooth passing of both money and property to the insured's heirs.

Can the ILIT last forever?

Depending upon state law, an irrevocable life insurance trust can last as long as any other trust, including dynasty trusts. If the ILIT is a dynasty-type ILIT, it will be subject to generation-skipping transfer taxes. (See Chapter 16, Protecting Future Generations—Dynasty Trusts.) Each person has a generation-skipping transfer tax exclusion. As a consequence of the generation-skipping transfer tax exclusion, life insurance premiums or other assets up to that amount can be placed in a dynasty ILIT without incurring any generation-skipping transfer tax. The generation-skipping transfer tax exclusion is applied against the amount contributed to the ILIT, not against the death proceeds of the insurance policy purchased by the ILIT. The ability to purchase life insurance inside of a dynasty ILIT provides significant leverage for the use of the generation-skipping transfer tax exclusion. For example, if the trustmaker contributed $100,000 to the Dynasty ILIT and that contribution was used to purchase a $1,000,000 insurance policy, at the death of the insured, the $1,000,000 insurance death benefit would be received by the ILIT without tax. The trustmaker would have only used $100,000 of his generation-skipping transfer tax exclusion, yet the ILIT would receive a death benefit of $1,000,000, all of which would qualify for the generation-skipping transfer tax exclusion.

Chapter 18

- Other Irrevocable Trusts -

In general terms there are really only two types of trusts: revocable trusts and irrevocable trusts. In general, the property held in revocable trusts will be included in your taxable estate (see Chapter 3, The Revocable Living Trust), and the property held in irrevocable trusts, if set up correctly, will not be included in your estate. We have already looked at several types of irrevocable trusts that take advantage of the fact the property held in an irrevocable trust will not be subject to estate tax upon your death (certain Special Needs Trusts in Chapter 8, certain Charitable Trusts in Chapter 10, certain Dynasty Trusts in Chapter 16 and all Irrevocable Life Insurance Trusts in Chapter 17). This chapter will give a brief overview of several other types of irrevocable trusts that might be useful tools in your specific situation. Your attorney can review your specific situation and your legacy planning goals and determine if any of these types of irrevocable trusts would be useful in your situation.

What is a Grantor Retained Annuity Trust?

A "Grantor Retained Annuity Trust" is a specific type of irrevocable trust that is actually set forth in the Internal Revenue Code. It is a favorite tool of the very wealthy, because it does not require the trustmaker to use up any gift tax or estate tax exemption amounts, but it can be very useful in other situations. In general, it works best if the trustmaker owns property that the trusmaker believes will significantly increase in value in the near future.

A GRAT works like this: the trustmaker creates the GRAT and contributes the chosen property to the trust. The trustee (which can be the trustmaker) then pays back to the trustmaker an "annuity payment" each year (or quarter, or month) for the length (or "term") of the trust from the trust assets. The trustmaker, within certain limits, can set both the amount of the annuity payment and the term of the trust, but the general goal is to make the total of the payments back to the trustmaker as low as the IRS regulations will allow. If set up correctly, at the end of the term of the trust, there will be some amount of property left in the trust, which can then go to the chosen beneficiaries (often the children) free of gift and estate tax.

The amount that the trustmaker must take out of the trust each year (or quarter, or month) without causing the transfer of property into the trust to cause gift or estate taxes must be carefully calculated according to the IRS regulations, and it depends entirely upon the interest rate that the Treasury Department must pay on a 10-year Treasury Bill at the most recent Treasury Bill auction. The actual calculations are too complex to go into in this brief overview, but the general rule is that the lower that interest rates are, the better the GRAT will work (i.e., more property will be left in the GRAT at the end of the GRAT term), so if you are in a low interest rate environment (such as we are when this chapter was written), you may want to consider using a GRAT.

What are the advantages of a GRAT?

The primary advantage, as noted above, is that if carefully constructed, a GRAT will not use up any of the trustmaker's gift tax exemption or estate tax exemption. Therefore, it is a favored tool for those who have already done other planning and have used up their entire gift tax exemption and still want to transfer property to loved ones free of gift and estate tax.

What are the disadvantages of a GRAT?

The primary disadvantage of a GRAT is that if the trustmaker dies during the term of the GRAT, all of the property in the GRAT will be included in the trustmaker's estate, so the GRAT will likely fail for the purpose intended, which was to transfer the property to other loved ones free of gift and estate taxes.

On the other hand, even if the trustmaker were to pass away during the term of the GRAT, there was no harmful effect of the GRAT, since the assets would have been included in the trustmaker's estate in any event.

What is a Qualified Personal Residence Trust?

A Qualified Personal Residence Trust ("QPRT") is another type of trust set forth in the Internal Revenue Code that is somewhat like a GRAT, but holds only a personal residence for a term of years, allowing the trustmaker of the trust to remain in the residence. When the term of the trust ends, ownership of the personal residence transfers to the beneficiaries of the trustmaker ("remainder beneficiaries").

The trustmaker can retain the right to rent the residence at fair market value after the term of the trust ends, but does have to pay the fair market rent if he or she wishes to remain in the residence after the term of the trust.

How Does It Work?

A QPRT takes advantage of certain provisions of the law to allow a gift to the QPRT by the trustmaker of his or her personal residence—for the ultimate benefit of the remainder beneficiaries, usually the children—at a discounted value. Either a principal residence or a vacation home can be transferred into a QPRT. This, in turn, will remove the asset from the trustmaker's estate, reducing potential estate taxes on the trustmaker's death.

For gift tax purposes, the original transfer will be treated as a gift to the remainder beneficiaries of the value of the future right to the residence at the end of the QPRT term ("remainder interest"). The trustmaker must file a gift tax return at the time the residence is transferred to the trust. The value of the remainder interest is derived by first determining the fair market value of the entire property, and then subtracting the value of the retained right of the trustmaker to live in the residence ("retained interest"). In general, the longer the term of the trust, the larger the value of the retained interest, the smaller the value of the remainder interest, and the smaller the taxable gift. If the trustmaker has not previously completely used his or her unified credit, the amount of gift tax due may be offset by the trustmaker's unified credit, thus possibly eliminating the need to pay any gift tax on the transfer of the residence to the QPRT.

If the trustmaker lives to the end of the specified period, the residence, including all post-gift appreciation, passes to remainder beneficiaries free of any additional federal or state estate or gift taxes. If the trustmaker dies before the end of the period, the value of the residence will be includible in the trustmaker's estate for estate tax purposes. The result would be the same had the trustmaker never created the QPRT.

What are the risks and complications?

If the trustmaker dies before the end of the QPRT term, the entire amount of property in the trust will be included in the trustmaker's taxable estate at its current value. Second, when the trustmaker set up the QPRT, he or she may have had to pay some gift tax. If any federal gift tax had to be paid, the trustmaker will have lost the use of that money for the term of the QPRT years.

Who pays the real estate taxes and maintenance expenses?

The trustmaker pays for all repairs to the house, utilities, lawn care and other basic maintenance, homeowner's insurance premiums, and real estate taxes. Such payments are for the benefit of the trustmaker as the tenant during the trust term and do not constitute taxable gifts.

Can the residence be sold?

A QPRT may allow for the sale of the residence. In addition, the trustee of the QPRT may hold the sales proceeds as long as the proceeds are held in a separate account. However, the residence may not be sold to the trustmaker, the trustmaker's spouse, or any entity controlled by the trustmaker or the trustmaker's spouse.

As a grantor trust, the grantor is treated as the owner of the property for federal income tax purposes. Therefore, all income, deductions, and credits associated with the property pass through the trust to the trustmaker of the trust. For the same reason, if the primary residence of the trustmaker is the subject property of a QPRT, the trustmaker qualifies for the $250,000 capital gain exclusion.

I have heard the term "Intentionally Defective Grantor Trust," what does that mean?

That term is popular, but it is misleading, since there is nothing "defective" about these types of trusts. The term came about because certain irrevocable trusts are drafted in such a way that the assets transferred into the trust will not be included in the trustmaker's estate for estate tax purposes, but so that the trustmaker will still be obligated to pay the income tax on any taxable income created by the trust. Because people initially thought that having the trustmaker pay the income tax on the trust's income was a bad thing, such a trust was "defective." Such a trust is termed a "grantor trust" by the Internal Revenue Service.

However, thoughtful trustmakers came to realize that if they were obligated to pay the income tax on the taxable income generated by the trust, it would allow the trust assets (which are outside the trustmaker's taxable estate) to grow much faster, which is a powerful estate planning technique, since the IRS has ruled that a trustmaker's payment of the income taxes incurred by the trust *is not* a form of gift by the trustmaker to the trust.

Therefore, nearly all trusts that can be set up as "grantor trusts" are set up in such a way, and there is nothing "defective" about those trusts. For example, by making a Dynasty Trust (see Chapter 16, Protecting Future Generations ~ Dynasty Trusts) a grantor trust, the trustmaker can help the Dynasty Trust grow much faster during the trustmaker's life, thereby greatly increasing the value of the Legacy for the future generations.

What happens if I don't want to pay the trust's income taxes anymore?

Luckily, the provisions of a grantor trust that cause the trustmaker to pay the income tax of the trust can be "turned off." So a trustmaker can set up an irrevocable trust as a grantor trust and pay the income taxes of the trust for so long as he or she wishes, but can "turn off" the grantor status of the trust at any time he desires, and from that point on the trust will pay its own income taxes out of the trust assets.

Unfortunately, this is a one-time-only opportunity. If a trust is set up as a grantor trust and the trustmaker "turns off" the grantor trust provisions, he or she cannot turn the grantor trust provisions back on again at a later date. In other words, from that point on the trust must pay its own income taxes and cannot transfer that obligation back to the trustmaker ever again.

Chapter 19

- Sorting Out What's Important -

The first time Alex and Amanda spoke with us they had one concern and that was to disinherit their 25-year-old son, Jason. Their two older children were doing fine, but about six months earlier Jason had dropped out of college in his third year to get married. In the heat of discussion, Jason had made it clear he no longer shared their values and wanted no more of their money. Heartbroken, Alex and Amanda had decided to arrange their estate plan to accommodate his wishes.

They had questions and uncertainties. Would Jason's new wife, Ellen, be entitled to anything from their sizable estate should Jason die? What about grandchildren? Alex and Amanda were hurting. They were reluctant to talk about their feelings with family members or friends. They had given plenty of thought about what they must do. They were now ready to make some hard choices. They wanted their decisions to be legal and enforceable.

We listened and tried to understand their hearts as well as their thoughts. Over a period of several meetings, we helped work through various alternatives and what they might look like. We counseled, but gave room for Alex and Amanda to work through their own solutions. Together we also helped address several other areas concerning their family and finances that they had not previously considered. In the meantime, their relationship with Jason and Ellen had softened. They decided against disinheritance and in favor of building wisdom into how all of their children's inheritances might be managed in ways that would achieve some clear objectives, using a living trust.

For Alex and Amanda, we were pleased to see that the decisions they reached were in favor of using their wealth as a bridge rather than a barrier to their relationships.

No One is Immune from Life's Unexpected Surprises

Nathan was an avid golfer and a natural athlete. Everyone who knew him liked him. His friends knew they could always call on him for help. He really cared about people. A brilliant businessman, he always seemed to have a large following of investors to go along with a growing real estate development enterprise. But he experienced what might be called a negative business downturn, and he and his partner were forced to cut corners and incur heavy debt. It was agonizing for Nathan to consider the possibility of his investors losing their savings. One afternoon while he, his wife, and four children were attending his son's baseball game, Nathan collapsed on the field and died from a massive heart attack. He was 37 years of age.

In many ways, young people are more vulnerable to life's unexpected surprises than older people. In the aftermath of his death, we helped his widow through the kinds of difficult times he had never imagined. Sadly, for a person who really cared about others and who often placed the interests of others above his own, estate planning for Nathan's family had just not been one of his priorities.

Planning for Those Who Can't Plan for Themselves

What a great day for family and friends! As Sally walked across the podium in her cap and gown, she paused to reflect briefly upon another important day in her life, ten years earlier, when at 12 years of age she received the news that both of her parents had been tragically killed in an automobile accident.

Although there was trauma following the loss of her parents, Sally remembered growing up being surrounded by extended family and friends. Surely there were many times of sadness and loneliness, but Sally also remembered a continuing feeling of comfort and security. Her parents had taken the proper steps to conscientiously plan for her future. Their instructions concerning Sally's care and well being had been clear and effective. Those entrusted with making important decisions on Sally's behalf had been carefully selected, and had all of the appropriate powers necessary to act without court intervention or expense. The estate assets, although modest in size, were conserved well and Sally did not need to take out student loans for her college education. She received her diploma that day with a broad smile on her face and thanks in her heart.

The most important things in life are not things. That day

brought added meaning to the love Sally's parents had for her, expressed in the planning they had done when she was a young child.

The Best Time to Plan

Always upbeat, Matt began his call with a funny story and usual talk of family and good things going on. In a casual way, as if to downplay its seriousness, Matt finally suggested that we should probably get together soon. He had just been diagnosed with a stage-four brain tumor. He was doing really well, he said. The news was just one of those things that happens and he wasn't afraid to die. Matt's main concern, he explained, was for his wife who he said was always the weak one. He said he wanted to get things in order for her and his kids. Stunned, and trying to voice an appropriate response, I offered to clear my calendar so the three of us could meet together as soon as possible. Matt promised to get back to me after checking with Sue for a good time for them.

In the months that followed I left messages on Matt's phone several times, puzzled as to why he had not called. At his memorial service Sue told me that at first they'd procrastinated, just not wanting to deal with the reality of their situation. Later, they'd become preoccupied with decisions concerning Matt's treatment. Things looked hopeful for a while, but in the final weeks approaching his death Matt became depressed and seemed to give up. They both knew they needed to do the necessary planning. But despite Sue's urging, Matt just couldn't seem to help with the financial and personal issues that she would need to deal with alone.

Planning for the future should never be postponed. That's especially true when life is clearly heading for a time of chaos, confusion and loss. Matt's inability to cope when he still could have taken the opportunity to do proper planning ended up being financially and emotionally disastrous to those he left behind. There is probably never as good a time as when you have the time to decide the things in life that really matter.

Mental Incapacity – an Essential Family Planning Issue

Waiting by their father's bedside, Sid's children had all finally arrived to be with him during these last days. He'd been well-cared for during the past three years, though dementia and other infirmities had certainly taken their toll. When it first became apparent that Sid was getting sick, the family got together and with our help affirmed some basic incapacity planning decisions that Sid and their mother, Nancy, had made a couple of years before. Bill, the middle child, was the one selected to take charge, mainly because the others trusted him and because he lived the closest of all of the children. Nancy had been well but not up to the task of making what seemed to be harder financial and health care decisions for Sid. Powers of attorney, decisions concerning life support, matters concerning privacy of medical information, and trust instructions concerning the parents' care during mental incapacity had all been essential in entirely avoiding court proceedings and unnecessary confusion and expense.

Five years earlier, Sid and Nancy had visited us concerning their affairs. They'd asked whether they should really have an estate plan given their assets were barely enough for their retirement. They never thought that their biggest concerns would occur during their lifetime rather than at death. Planning for the possibility of mental incapacity turned out to be a very good decision for them.

People are living longer, but not necessarily healthier, lives. It is more likely now than ever that for a married couple at least one will experience a prolonged period of significant mental incapacity. Planning well for this eventuality is essential. Regardless of the size of your estate, it is critical to plan for the growing possibility of mental incapacity.

The Importance of Funding and Updating

Sylvia and John were a young married couple, each with children from previous marriages, who wanted to make sure their affairs were in order. We recommended a trust and other planning tools for their blended family. As is typical in our practice, we counseled them about the funding aspects of implementing their trust. For them, funding consisted of making correct beneficiary designations and titling their assets in a way that would be consistent with their estate plan—so that in the event of death or incapacity the provisions they'd created would actually work. We followed through to make sure the titling was done correctly, and convinced Sylvia and John to agree to visit with us regularly to review and make sure their planning was updated.

Despite our urging over the years, we didn't hear from

Sylvia until ten years later. John had recently died. It seemed that at some point John had taken a $1 million life insurance policy naming his son from his previous marriage as beneficiary. We needed to open a probate court proceeding to govern the proceeds for the benefit of the son. Sylvia and the other children were not entitled to any of the insurance benefits. John's son, who was currently dealing with drug problems, would be entitled to receive the proceeds on his 21st birthday.

Had Sylvia and John had followed through to meet, review and update their estate plan, we would have counseled John differently. Even if he had wanted to include life insurance provisions for his son in his planning, we would have advised him at the very least to name his trust as beneficiary. That way the court proceeding could have been avoided and the proceeds could have been held in trust for his son's benefit until he was older and until he had recovered from the drug issues.

To make sure your estate plan will actually work as intended, proper funding is necessary from the beginning. Just as important is to have your plan and funding decisions reviewed and updated regularly.

INDEX